Goodbye Mr Ex

A woman's guide to moving on

Marina Pearson

Goodbye Mr Ex

First published in 2013 by

Ecademy Press

48 St Vincent Drive, St Albans, Herts, AL1 5SJ, UK
info@ecademy-press.com
www.ecademy-press.com

Book layout by Neil Coe.
Edited by: Wendy Millgate from Wendy With Words.

Printed on acid-free paper from managed forests. This book is printed on demand to fulfill orders, so no copies will be remaindered or pulped.

ISBN 978-1-908746-62-7

A CIP catalogue record for this book is available from the British Library.

This book is available online and in all good bookstores.

Dedication

I want to dedicate this book to my close family: mum, dad and my two sisters and to all of those women going through heartbreaking times.

Testimonials

"Marina has found the ideal way to support you in transforming a painful ending of your marriage into a great start for the rest of your life. For all the women out there that just turned single, it is the most practical and inspiring book to get your life back on track and to find happiness again."

Marie Diamond, Transformational Leader and Feng Shui Master, featured in The Secret

"The book is so refreshing – it feels like it's part of a growing school of modern thought in the grand tradition of the Stoics, my favourite philosophers! I love the blend of gentle yet firm support. It's not tough love to me; it's nurturing necessity. I thought the combo was magic."

Natasha Phillips, Researching Reform

"An honest and plain-English guide to how to stop your ex – or how you react to your ex – getting in the way of a beautiful life. Just like her workshops, Marina's book is engaging and accessible, yet does not dumb down the powerful effects of a break-up on the heart and spirit, nor the good that can come from learning how to shift through your divorce and break-up, leaving bitterness way behind you."

Suzy Miller, Founder of Divorce In A Box

Transform your ex relationship struggle into freedom

Ever wondered what keeps most women struggling in the pain and anger of their ex-relationships and why they keep having their buttons pushed? This book identifies what these factors are and will give you a pro-active approach to free you from your past in a quick and painless fashion, giving you back your "inner mojo" and a sense of peace, so you can move on without looking back.

Why struggle and go it alone when you don't have to? Free yourself of the past today and create your new life!

Acknowledgements

I would very much like to acknowledge all my teachers such as Doctor John Demartini and Clinton Swaine who have taught me so much along my personal development journey and have been key players in furthering my growth, even though it may have felt VERY uncomfortable for me.

I also want to acknowledge my mentor, and somebody that I can now call a dear friend, Deri Llewellyn-Davies, who has had the patience of a saint while seeing me through the journey of my business. And Marie Diamond for believing in me, seeing my potential and for clearing the energy in my home so that the words would flow.

I would also like to thank my good friends Christiane Pedros, Angelique Tsang, Emma Cummings, Richard Cash, Andrew Gray, Stephanie Burton, Sidra Jafri, Natasha Caton and Caroline Ainslie for believing in my work and being there for me professionally and personally when challenges have come my way.

To my Key Person of Influence accountability group for cheering me on when I got somewhat distracted and off-track. And to Mindy and her team—Neil and Emma—without who I wouldn't be able to actually get this book out there and deliver what I believe is a message that needs to be heard. I would also like to say a thank you to Wendy my editor who was incredible during the whole process and Andrew Priestley for the fabulous illustrations in the book. To Kim Jobst for guiding me towards my purpose and for keeping me in good health so that I had the energy to write the book.

And to all my lovely ladies that contributed their personal stories to provide the book's content so other women could be inspired to take action.

And finally to my beloved Marc—my soulmate and best friend—without who I don't know where I would be. Thank you sweetie.

Preface

I have created this book with the intention of reaching out to women who, like I once did, are struggling to get over their past relationships, possibly because of a messy divorce or a heart wrenching break-up. Having been through a divorce back in 2006 and a significant number of break-ups, I struggled for many years to get over most of them, while not understanding why it was taking so long. I often played out very negative emotions and patterns of behaviour towards myself and others to block out the pain. Each break-up left a tiny bit of myself behind, to the point where I didn't really know who I was anymore, or what I wanted. I would go into new relationships and the same old patterns would just happen again.

Now that I'm at the other end, finally content in my own skin, in a place of gratitude for my past and have found myself in a fantastic relationship, I want to help you find the same, if that's what you want!

I wish this book had been around when I was going through each of my break-ups and divorce. I might have saved myself the years of unnecessary pain, of addiction, self-abuse and suicidal tendencies. However, that was not the path that I was supposed to follow. Instead, I struggled month after month, year after year, to let go of my pain and the relationships with each of my exes.

I have studied countless courses and programmes in my quest for knowledge to empower me and other women to move on from our exes and create a new story. But the best learning has been through my own experience. In this book I am transparent about my own course with my exes—yes, there **were** a few—so yes, I get you and yes, I've been there. I've dealt with cheating (from both sides), break-ups by email, divorce, depression, suicide attempts and being left on my own to fend for myself. Now, thankfully, I'm on the other side with great relationships with my exes, my family and my dream partner.

It took a long time of learning for me to know what I know now, and that is that I wouldn't be the person I am today without my experiences with each of my exes. Each of them pushed me towards loving myself more and more. The more challenging it got, the more I grew and the faster I moved towards being happy, confident and successful. I would even go as far to say that each and every one of them was my spiritual teacher.

Now, I know that might be hard for some of you to swallow. My ex, my spiritual teacher? Him? What a load of crap... But bear with me here...

Did my exes give me some tough love? Yes! ... But without that, I believe I would never have grown the way I have.

Has it been uncomfortable? Hell yes!

Have there been tears? Of course there have.

But has it been worth it?

Yes, yes, yes!

But I am only able to see this now and fully experience *gratitude* for my divorce, and the tough times I had with my exes, because I have learnt some incredible tools along the way. My insatiable curiosity and need to heal from my divorce and past have taken me on a journey of personal development that started in 2007. Never did I think back then that I would be in the happy, committed relationship I find myself in today.

Thanks to applying the tools that I now share with you in this book, and of course through my commitment to changing myself, it has been possible to not only heal and grow, but to also attract my dream relationship.

I now coach women through getting over their exes, and I run programmes to do the same, through my business, my passion. I have seen all sorts of shifts with my clients, and have seen them turn their perceived nightmare into a beautiful gift. They no longer have to struggle with their lack of confidence and their pain. Instead, they have reclaimed their power and sense of who they truly are.

This is why I decided to write this book—as a testimony that, yes, all this is possible! You can transform the anger, guilt, hurt and jealousy that you may be feeling (towards him in this moment and/or when you see him), into a sublime inner peace that can create an abundant amount of prosperity for yourself and your loved ones.

I believe, I know, there is another way, and somehow you must too, otherwise you would not be reading this book. Healing is an inevitable part of the journey, but it doesn't need to be something you fear. In fact, the rewards are priceless. I truly believe that if I hadn't taken the time to focus on me and releasing the past, I wouldn't be in the relationship I find myself in now. To have what you want, you will need to work towards it. Nothing was ever achieved without putting the effort in.

So thank you for allowing me now, through this book, to join with you and help you on your journey as you move on from your ex.

Contents

Introduction

So you have an ex? What do you *really* feel, deep down, when you say those words—'my ex'. Relief (Thank God it's over!)? Sadness? Anger (Due to the past or he's still around, pushing your buttons)? Regret? Shame? Longing for what was (or your fantasy of what was)? Perhaps nothing, as you've pushed it all down, deep down... There's this blank emptiness...Emotional bankruptcy.

There's another word that can bring up similar images and feelings—'break-up'. Yes, something really BREAKS during a break-up, doesn't it? And it's not just the relationship. The people involved—YOU and your ex—may feel broken, in mind and heart, and guess what? It even it takes its toll on your body. Throw in a few break-ups and a few exes and you're in for a rollercoaster ride that you never seem to get off.

You may be lucky and sail through the break-up, or you may find you feel like you're in little tiny pieces, for quite a while. I know I did. How do we deal with this 'broken-ness'? Well, sometimes we don't at first, and in walks depression, confusion, anger, blame ... then comes the sabotage to avoid the pain—over- or under-eating, poor food choices, too much alcohol, too many smokes, being reclusive OR the opposite, going nuts and over-partying and sleeping with just one man too many!

You may be lucky and go into another relationship. Yay! You deserve it ... AT LAST! But what many women find (and I did too!) is you just attract the same sort of guy and the same sort of relationships and patterns (both yours and his) once more. Here we go around the mulberry bush—again!

Well, you deserve better than that. We all do. There is always something ticking away, pushing us to move on, to seek communion with another soul in a beautiful and growing way, and we can do it. We just need help in how to move on from the past effectively, to learn new ways of being and doing, so that we can come out the other end feeling at peace and healthy within ourselves—with healthy self-love, healthy patterns of communication, healthy expectations, and best of all, feeling gratitude.

But I'm here to say that you have to deal with what's going on inside you and find that peace within, to resolve the inner conflict with your ex and to move on BEFORE you go out looking for (or attracting) another partner again. You deserve to be given the best chance of finding that happiness and contentment you yearn for. And this is where this books comes in ...

Congratulations on picking up this book and giving yourself the opportunity to discover how you can finally move on from your ex, once and for all. It's time to break free from the anger, resentment and hurt, so you can be at peace and can move forward to create the type of life and relationships you have dreamed of ... to be free of the past at last.

Imagine...

... a world where you no longer are bogged down with the conflict; where you don't feel stressed anymore from missing him; you're not still feeling hurt; and you have let go of the anger at things, like how he doesn't keep his word and keeps changing things around. What would this world look like for you?

Imagine how different your world and that of your children (if you have them) would be if everything was as you wished it would be, right now.

And then ... imagine finally making space for that new relationship—the one you've dreamed about!

The truth is that unless you work on the past, you will not be able to attract the man you desire or be present in the next relationship.

If you follow the steps in the book, it is possible to work on your past proactively and quickly to create that future world and relationship you just imagined. I know this because it happened in my own life—there is nothing in this book that I have not experienced myself. I never imagined I would ever get to the point where my ex-husband and I would end up communicating again. Nor did I ever expect to overcome a relationship that ended only a year ago. Nor did I think I would ever again speak to one ex who was so angry he shut off communication with me for six months. Nevertheless, all of this happened, and more, by taking the steps through *The S.H.I.F.T. Model* that I lay out for you here in this book.

Furthermore, I have seen similar results time and time again with my coaching clients. Having worked with clients through the processes within *The S.H.I.F.T. Model*, I have seen some incredible shifts where they were able to let go of obsessing over their ex, become friends with him even and commence their new dating journey—all in a very short amount of time.

There is a common belief that healing from an ex-relationship takes a long time—that it can take years, in fact. But I know that it doesn't *have* to be so. If you work with a program, like this one, it does not need to take an eternity for things to change.

Your wounds will determine your destiny, as they will be reflected in the choices you make and the actions you take. By using the combination of techniques that I have learnt along the way, and that I use with my clients, you will make new choices, take new actions and become *unstuck in no time. You will start to feel lighter and more at peace.*

Perhaps you've experienced other counselling methods, spending hours going over and over the past—that's what I did too. You're not alone there. But did you find, like me and many others, that traditional 'talk therapy' can take a long time to work—if at all? I know some friends who are still going to talk to their therapist three years on; however, I know without a doubt that a new proactive approach, such as this program, would have moved them forward much more quickly. One of my clients testified that she got more out of one session using the techniques that I use in the book than she had got out of four years of therapy.

I am not knocking the traditional 'talk therapy'—I went to counselling myself for years after my divorce and at the time I saw the value in talking about my ex. My psychotherapist seemed to be one of the few people who would listen to me, and as you know, being listened to is very important. *But* I am knocking on its head the notion that recovery has to take a long, long time. Years on, I now realize that if I had continued going, I would not have seen the changes that I have experienced as a result of using the techniques laid out before you in this book.

Thankfully, these days a lot of the complementary therapies that were once considered a bit 'woo-woo' are now being talked about in mainstream media and are being backed up by scientific research. This is exciting, as new forms of personal development are speeding up the process of healing, meaning that people can more quickly reduce their state of suffering.

As I speak of us challenging old notions, let's briefly debunk what I have identified as the top three relationship myths and clarify some key points, so that you have a better understanding of where this book is coming from.

De-bunking the most popular relationship myths

✗ MYTH:
Love is only about support.

✓ TRUTH:
Love is a balance of support and challenge.

Love is about being supported and challenged at the same time. The love that we are sometimes exposed to in movies does not exist. That is definitely the fairy tale version. Love has both a negative and positive aspect to it. Now, I know that you are probably thinking *Marina, are you mad?* and my answer is "No".

I have lots of friends who have children and there are days their children really challenge them, and there are days that the kids behave themselves and are like angels. Do their parents love them? Sure they do. Are their kids sometimes challenging them and sometimes supporting them? Yes, they are. The same will go for your ex. He will challenge you and be supporting you at the same time. Love is about balance. If you were just supported all the time, you wouldn't grow or evolve. I know it's maybe tough to get your head around this, but by the end of the book you will understand what I mean.

✗ *MYTH:*
Relationships are all about happiness.

✓ *TRUTH:*
Relationships are also about growth, not only happiness.

Relationships are not only here to make you happy; they are here to make you grow and learn about who you are. This is crucial to understand. Why? Because if you are setting happiness as the benchmark for your relationship's success, you will feel very disappointed and wonder why relationships are hard or why they don't work. Because we all know that no one is happy in a relationship 100 per cent of the time.

However, if you set *growth* as a benchmark for your relationship's success, you will probably find that you have a lot of relationship success. As the old adage says: "***If you are not growing, you are dying." So why not use this time to grow and evolve?***

✗ *MYTH:*
Your partner in a happy relationship is committed to what is important to YOU!

✓ *TRUTH:*
Partners in a relationship are firstly committed to what is important to them and not to you.

People commit to relationships based on whether their values are being ticked or, even better, shared by their partner. If they feel that what is important to them is being supported, they will stay. If what is highly important to them is being challenged, they will either stray or leave permanently.

For example, if a man believes that his wife doesn't appreciate his financial contribution towards the family, or that she is being challenged by the fact he doesn't contribute enough to what she finds important (for instance, spending time with the family), then chances are one of them will stray, as neither is being appreciated for contributing to what the other finds important.

Being aware of these myths will help you understand what relationships are truly about. In this way your perspective will widen and unrealistic expectations will decrease, thereby lessening possible disappointment.

There are other myths besides the ones listed above, which are discussed in more detail during my *Goodbye Mr Ex* audio and video programmes.

7 key factors that keep you struggling

Aside from the myths, I have identified seven key things that women do, or don't do, that will keep them stuck in the pain and anger, stopping them from moving on.

I have found that when my clients either come to me or the workshops I have hosted, they are in the struggle because:

1. they are not committed to letting go—they would prefer to be right and hang onto their fears;

2. they judge themselves and their ex, which keeps them angry and jealous;
3. they re-hash the same story over and over, which renders them powerless and keeps them obsessing;
4. they make massive assumptions about their ex and hold unrealistic expectations, which keeps them disappointed and frustrated;
5. they use language that blames and shames their ex, which keeps them in the conflict with their ex and themselves;
6. they keep wishing they had done things differently, which keeps them in guilt and are very worried about what will happen in the future, which keeps them in the fear; and/or
7. they surround themselves with the wrong support either because they falsely believe that family and friends are the best people to talk to; or seek no outside support as they believe that doing it on their own will be just fine.

Can you identify with any of these behaviours above?

The S.H.I.F.T. Model: A 7-step process to lift you out of struggle

To address each of these mistakes I have created a 7-step process—*The S.H.I.F.T Model*—to support you to Express (Part 1), Release (Part 2) and Move On (Part 3) from your ex, which will leave you feeling cared for and empowered. Each chapter in this book addresses one of these steps.

The 7 Steps that will help you S.H.I.F.T. are:

1. Find your WHY so you can **Commit**
2. **See** your ex as a reflection of you, so you can replace judgement with feelings of wholeness
3. **Heal** your conscious and unconscious stories to transform your feelings of powerlessness to powerfulness
4. **Inquire** to transform your disappointments into insights
5. **Focus** to change your inner conflicts into softness
6. **Transform** your regret of the past and fear of the future into feelings of gratitude
7. **Support** and share, so you no longer have to go it alone and struggle.

Where are you now?

When followed, the process of *The S.H.I.F.T Model* will guide you on a journey from your head into your heart. This journey is so short yet can take a life-time to experience. Some don't ever get there, but with *The S.H.I.F.T. Model* my hope is your journey will be quickened. The trick is to reach that place in your heart, so you can experience that release and freedom for yourself.

On this journey I have identified three stages that exist to getting over him.

Beginning stage:
Grief/Shock—Just broken up/divorced

If you are here, in this beginning stage, you will be currently experiencing a range of emotions that seem to bounce from one end of the spectrum to the other. I call this the *Yo-yo Syndrome*. You spend most of your day missing him and wanting him back, and the other half, angry at him for having done x, y and z. You may not be able to eat or sleep. You may be telling everybody about what he has done or not done. You somehow feel that if he were to ask you to come back that you would, even though you know it's wrong for you—but anything would better than where you are at now. This is when your emotions are at their most intense and your life seems to be consumed by them.

Middle Stage: Acceptance—Getting on, but your buttons are still being pushed

You may be at the stage where you are just getting on with it, the intensity of the emotions has died down and you are now able to focus a bit better than you could before; however, you still get triggered (become emotionally affected) by things like the music you used to listen to together, or places that you used to visit. You may still get your buttons pushed when, and if, you see him. He irritates you and somehow your day is ruined because he shows up and aggravates your mood. You are still not able to thank him for being in your life and accept what has happened and there is still some resentment there. Most women live here. The truth is that if you are still living here, he will run you still, and this will be causing stress in your system.

Last Stage: Gratitude—You wouldn't change a thing

Only a very small number get to this last stage of gratitude. In fact, I would say that the majority fending for themselves out there don't *ever* experience this feeling. Until you can actually shut your eyes and just feel or say "Thank you, I love you" then you are not over him. I want you to do that right now.

EXERCISE:

Close your eyes and imagine that your ex is standing right in front of you. Can you honestly say, with hand on heart, "Thank you, I love you"? Give it a go.

Now do it for every single ex. The feeling you should get here is one of complete serenity, where, if somebody asked you, "Would you change anything of the past?" you would say "No". This is the end of your journey.

Did you find that hard to do? If you did, that's normal. After all, this is the final stage—the final goal. When you are 100 per cent free and have completely moved on, you will be in a space of gratitude. There seems to be a lot of confusion between acceptance and gratitude, and it's not until you reach that place of gratitude that you know that you are truly over him. You will know when you have arrived because you will finally believe that you wouldn't have changed a thing about the past.

So which stage are you at?

The great thing is that the steps I take you through in this book to say goodbye to your ex can be used either at the beginning stage or the middle stage to move you towards finally saying goodbye and feeling grateful.

You're going to find some exercises and processes throughout that will get you started immediately, and there are also case studies—real life experiences of clients using the *S.H.I.F.T. Model* —that you will find informative and very motivating. I also share quite candidly my own ex experiences. As I shared in the preface, I've 'been there and done that', 'got the T-Shirt' and this is the book. My journey has involved break-ups and a divorce, being on an emotional rollercoaster with them all. So to give you a heads-up, here's a quick snapshot of my ex-journey. (By the way, the names of my exes have been changed for privacy, of course):

- Ex-husband – relationship ended 2006
- George – proper relationship ended towards the end of 2010 but on and off encounters for 10 years
- Paul – relationship ended towards the middle of 2011
- Fiancé – August 2011 – present day

But before I take you on this journey, I want you to imagine that you are an Explorer Extraordinaire. Treat this book as your handbook to get you from point A, which is where you are now, to point B, which is where you will end up at your destination—*a place where you are at peace and can create a different world for yourself.*

Some of the things I talk about may well press your buttons, which is great, because it means that I am challenging your usual reality that has kept you stuck in the past. At times you may not like what I have to say, and that is great too. Be open to exploring that feeling as we go, and get curious about why it has pushed a button.

You may be asking yourself why it has taken this long to finally address the challenges you face with your ex. Well, in *Chapter 1: Commit*, I will be delving into understanding your resistance and what to do about it, so that if, at any point, it comes up again, you will know what to do to keep on moving forward.

So it is time to lighten the load that has been holding you down for so long, to finally unpack it and leave it behind!

Don't worry; I will be holding your hand throughout.

PART 1: EXPRESS

COMMIT

"There's a difference between interest and commitment. When you're interested in doing something, you do it only when circumstances permit. When you're committed to something, you accept no excuses, only results."

Art Turock

Usually, the number one reason why women find it so hard to move on is *because they were **never committed** to doing so.* Without taking this step, you are guaranteed to stay stuck.

Before my clients come to me, I always ask them the question: "Are you ready to let go of all the negative emotions that you are currently harbouring?" If the answer that comes out is not 100 per cent, I know they are not ready to move on yet.

Lack of commitment is like having one foot on the dock and one foot on the boat. By not committing to either the dock or the boat, you are stuck in the middle, not going anywhere and putting a lot of energy in propping yourself up so you don't fall into the water.

Wouldn't it be easier to just commit to one or the other? Staying or getting on the boat? Not making a decision is what keeps you in the turmoil and pain. Without fully committing to your journey to express, release and move on, you will stay where you are.

What true commitment looks like

Put your head underwater and keep it there for a while and you'll soon realize that you are 100 per cent committed to breathing.

- Notice that you don't make excuses so as not to breathe.
- Notice that you don't worry about motivating yourself to breathe.
- Notice that you don't need to justify your desire to breathe.

You just breathe. *Commitment is action.* No excuses. No debate. No lengthy analysis. No whining about how hard it is. No worrying about what others might think. No cowardly delays. Just go. Just do.

What if something gets in the way of your commitment? What would you do if someone prevented you from breathing?

I am not saying to *really* stick yourself under water, of course. I just want to give you a tangible sense of what commitment looks and feels like. Commitment will make you unstoppable, but it always starts with the decision: "Yes, I am committed." And in our case here, it is: "Yes, I am committed to letting go."

Moving on and un-sticking yourself from your ex takes commitment and the good news is that it all starts with a choice. *The buck stops here if you choose to do the work* to move on from him. I cannot reiterate this enough. With the right choices, you can finally release the stress and get off the emotional rollercoaster.

The thing to know is that your situation in the outer world will not change if your inner world doesn't. So you need commitment to work on the inner, and part of that commitment is having a big enough WHY (a big enough reason to let go). We all create our own realities, which are founded in our perceptions—the meanings we give to things, our belief systems, what we deem important, our environment, fears and our patterns. If you decide you want to change them, you will find yourself in a **new chapter of your life, feeling free and claiming your own power back**.

Now, that's a pretty big WHY, right? But you'd be surprised at how many women don't want to let go, and we'll look at all the excuses soon. But now, let's look at **what happens when you choose NOT to take a proactive approach**, because in there you will find some really BIG WHYs.

What happens if you choose not to take a proactive approach and make a commitment to move on...?

At any point when you harbour hurt, anger, jealousy or shame, you are giving your power to your ex, and giving permission for each of these negative emotions to live in your head, without permission, like a squatter. There they will hang out and drive your thoughts and feelings and sap your energy. If you don't fully express these emotions, you are exposing yourself to a constant range of negative emotions, the energy of which remain stuck in your body, placing your body under constant stress as the message is sent that you are in danger. This will lead to mental, emotional and physical illness. Let me explain some more.

When under incessant stress your body rallies and remains constantly in survival/ protection or what is called 'repair' mode. When you are stressed and your body remains in protection mode, what happens is your organism will close itself down by increasing the adrenalin in your body, which in turn will increase your levels of cortisol. Cortisol is a hormone produced by the adrenal gland as a part of your daily hormonal cycle. Cortisol increases blood sugar levels, increases blood pressure and suppresses the immune system.

If the immune system is suppressed, this means it can't do its job properly and your body cannot protect itself from illness and disease which stops it from healing, which is hugely detrimental on your well-being. For example, at some point, what often happens after a constant period of stress is you blow out your adrenals, leading to fatigue and thyroid problems. As it is highly toxic, too much cortisol in the body on a consistent basis can lead to weight gain and memory loss.

For your body to heal, it needs to be in *growth mode* and that can only happen if your immune system is functioning properly and you are feeling relaxed and at peace. There is much more involved in remaining in growth mode and that forms one of the keys steps of the *S.H.I.F.T. Model*: *Healing your Unconscious Story*, which comprises your inner beliefs and thoughts. You'll learn more on how to do this in Chapter 4.

Some decide to take the easy road, but I can tell you repressing negative feelings with cigarettes and alcohol will not help. It will ultimately make matters worse. Yes, you may want to numb the pain, but it will come back and bite you. If you feel and express your emotions, you will then expel the negative energy, which will give you your vitality back. What is interesting is that each different emotion like anger or guilt or jealousy will reside in different parts of the body.

The diagram will give you a clearer idea of how these negative emotions are affecting your body and where they live.

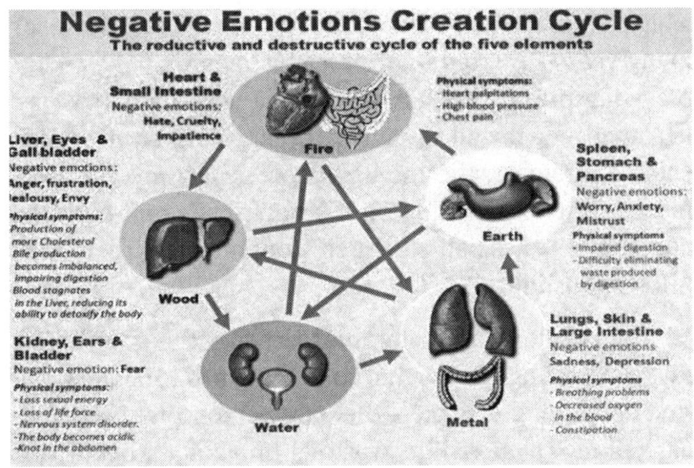

I have first-hand experience of this with my mother, who, as I write this, has a degenerative disease called 'cortical basal degeneration'. She was diagnosed with it when she was fifty-six and she is now seventy-two. Degenerative diseases are usually caused by a genetic mutation. Now, a genetic mutation doesn't just appear. To expose the body to something like that must have meant that her body was pushed to its optimum capacity.

My perception of my mother, even from a young age, was that she was always busy and stressed out. When I was born, my mother was already on her second marriage, as the first became too difficult and painful. By marrying my dad, she married somebody who was twenty-one years her senior, which brought with it its own complications, which exacerbated her feelings of loneliness and stress.

Now, all of these goings-on, of course, had a direct impact on me. I was there with her while she was in that stressed-out state. Her fears, anxieties and the pain that she felt, as well as her interaction with my father, all played a big part in the way I felt about myself. Unfortunately, for many years I carried a lot of anger towards her for this, believing that it was her fault that I was the way I was. I blamed her for all my insecurities and even my failed suicide attempts, the intense depressions, my anorexia, my patterns of cheating on my boyfriends and my drug addictions—these all stemmed from my inability to take full responsibility.

As an adult, I was finally able to let all of this go and start my own healing. I knew that something had to change, and that something was me—the only person that went into each of my relationships was me! I now don't blame her, or my father, in any way. I have made peace with it all and am eternally grateful I had the parents I did. I would not change my past in any way. I am who I am today because of my history, *but it is history and is not my present.*

I share this family story with you as an illustration of how holding onto past hurts cannot only affect you, but also how it can affect your children. If you decide to get pregnant in the future then please consider this:

> "Who you are and what you're like when you're pregnant will affect who that baby is", says Janet DiPietro, a developmental psychologist at John Hopkins University. "Women's psychological functioning during pregnancy -- their anxiety level, stress, personality -- ultimately affects the temperament of their babies. It has to ... the baby is awash in all the chemicals produced by the mom." [1]

1 Fetus To Mom: You are Stressing Me Out, Medicine.Net.com
http://www.medicinenet.com/script/main/art.asp?articlekey=51730&page=2

It's amazing how anxieties and patterns are handed down from generation to generation without us even realising.

All I want for you is for you to take care of yourself. Your history is your present and you are constantly reminded of that. It is hard and I truly get that.

I don't have children with any of my exes but my sisters do, and I know the struggles that they have had to endure as a result. As mentioned before, I was witness to my mother's struggle, so I know how hard it can get sometimes. But I encourage you to tune into and acknowledge what you are feeling and find a constructive way to express it. Give the following activity a go:

EXERCISE: Tantrum Off

The best way to feel what you feel is to tune into the feeling and feel it ... *Really feel it*. Then, shout and scream, or take a bat and hit a pillow. Hit that pillow until you cannot do it anymore. It really works.

Go on – go into a park today and scream and shout at the top of your lungs or get that pillow and whack it a few times!

I was at a workshop a few years back and I was asked to express rage. I honestly didn't know what it was, but I went for it anyway. Suddenly, all this anger and rage and hurt welled up and I started screaming and shouting, tears running down my face everywhere. I had honestly never felt that alive! I felt so much electricity running through my body.

After ten minutes of screaming and raging, I felt so much lighter! I felt as if years had come off me. It was as if a layer of my being had just dropped off. I experienced this again last year at the Enlightened Warrior Camp and once again I felt that I had lost two kilos worth of baggage. Lighter, more present and such a sense of peace.

Even though shouting on your own in a field or park might feel odd, it will make you feel a whole lot better and will guarantee to make you feel alive, while giving you back vital energy.

Reasons for staying stuck

So why is it that you would want to stay where you are, either staying in the negative relationship you are in or hanging onto the memory of it, if there are so many detrimental implications to not doing something about your situation? What I have discovered along the way is that *there is a perception that there will be more drawbacks to letting go than benefits* and this usually stems from a number of fears.

Below are the most common fears that that I have come across when I speak to potential clients that stop them from moving forward.

1. *Fear of being alone*

To finally let go of having their ex push their buttons, and to release all the anger, resentment and hurt, means finally having to *confront being alone*, which for some can be very scary. You may be thinking to yourself that he was the best thing that ever happened to you and that finding somebody that good won't be possible? Well, the truth is that this thought is not true. You will just need to put your efforts into healing and working through your emotions. By clearing out the old, you will bring in someone very new, who will be better for you. You can always use your exes as benchmarks to see how far you have come!

Maybe it is scary for you at the moment, but one thing is guaranteed: If you are still looking back and not being present to what is going on around you, and not planning for the future, you may miss the chance of being in another, better relationship.

There is nothing to fear, other than fear itself. Fear is a projection of something that has not happened. Unless you have a crystal ball, you don't know what is ahead of you.

Maybe this is the time for you to follow your heart and open yourself up to new experiences that will help you soar. I have seen this time and time again with clients. Moving on for them has given them their life back.

2. *Fear of loss*

There is also the fear that if they finally let him and the emotions go, they will not be close to him anymore. Now, I know what you are thinking: *But Marina, why would I want him close if I am still angry and hurting?* Well, it's an interesting one—there are some women who, even in the anger, still want the closeness because they feel guilty or uncomfortable about living for themselves.

However, I want to let you know that living for yourself is the best thing you can ever do! Now, I know this may be scary. When I have spoken to broken-hearted women, I often hear that they feel lost and without direction. They somehow lost who they were in the relationship, and this is perfectly normal. Research shows that *when two people become a couple, the brain extends its idea of self to include the other; instead of the slender pronoun "I", a plural self emerges, who can borrow some of the other's assets and strengths.*[2]

2 Ackerman, Dian, The Brain On Love, New York Times http://opinionator.blogs.nytimes.com/2012/03/24/the-brain-on-love/, March 24, 2012

If you are struggling to move on, you can always turn this time into a discovery of who you are and what is waiting out there for you.

3. *Fear of losing part of their identity*

I have often heard (and have felt it myself) that letting go of the past and your ex can be likened to a death, which can be very painful. It is like saying goodbye to a part of yourself and a life that was full of so much promise, but that now cannot be.

Saying goodbye to this part of who you are may be scary, as the question that comes at us is "Who am I now and who would I be without my ex pushing my buttons?"

All I can say is that *you would be you!* You are not your relationship. The beautiful you that is here and waiting for you to commit to your own path, wherever it may lead. You have the choice to enjoy your own adventure and journey.

4. *Fear of trusting the process*

There may be a certain lack of trust that things will turn out okay. However, if you do decide to commit to letting go, *it will turn out to be okay. You will be fine* if you take action and take the time to heal.

I have successfully gone through many break-ups, as have my clients, and the one thing that all my clients, and I, have in common is that we trusted in the process. We trusted that if we actually took a proactive approach, we would get through it, and we did.

5. *Fear of losing*

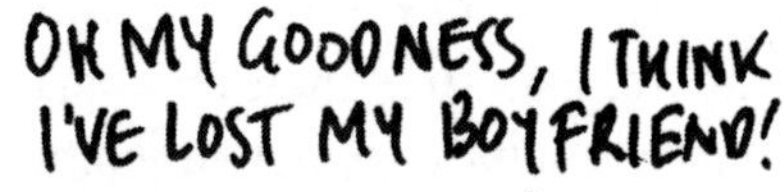

I have often seen women who think that if they commit to their journey of letting go, that somehow their ex-partner has won; but this is not the case! He will definitely win if you don't.

It seems that, for many, being right is more important than the will to be happy. There is an old adage that you can be right or you can be happy, but you cannot be both. But wanting to be right and holding onto this feeling—this fear of losing—will keep you stuck.

What if you decided today that letting go of being right would have you win? *What if winning was about letting go?* By making the commitment, you are saying "I win" because you can now release all the negative emotions.

Releasing and moving on takes action and commitment, it takes 'doing the work'. It doesn't need to be hard toil. My clients and I have a lot of fun together doing the process and the great thing is that they feel safe, knowing that they are going to reach their goal, no matter what.

6. *Fear of the unknown*

Another reason why women don't fully commit to letting go is because holding onto the anger and resentment becomes a normal state of affairs. What I have experienced within myself, and in others as well, is that there is a *belief* that 'it's better to have the discomfort than *not know* what comes after it.'

Maybe this is where you are at the moment. If so, all I can say is that what awaits you on the other side is peace of mind, a sense of calmness and a feeling of gratitude that was not there before. I know because I have experienced it myself and I see this every time I work with my clients.

Change can be very scary for the unconscious, and as the unconscious side of our brain runs 95 per cent of what we do, if we are met with an opportunity to change, it will start to feel unsafe. The problem with staying in the comfort zone is that *life actually starts beyond it!*

7. *Fear of facing the pain*

There is a common belief that letting go is a painful process and that facing your demons will be worse or harder than where you are now. However, this is not true. Are you not *already* getting your buttons pushed by your ex? Are you not *already* feeling the emotions? *Are you not already feeling the pain?*

The fact is that the can of worms is already open and the only thing waiting for you on the other side of where you are now is peace—*peace of mind and presence.*

8. *Fear of what others will think*

This is a very popular one, among women who know that the relationship is not right for them, but who don't leave because they fear hurting their ex and fear the opinion of others.

Guilt is a funny thing but it will keep you captive and will not let you listen to your heart. If you find yourself in this situation, all I will say is this – if you are not happy in the relationship, the chances are that your ex wont be either – so wouldn't it be better to just say goodbye and live your life by what is right for you?

I guarantee that in years to come, nobody will be thanking you for staying in a relationship that wasn't right for you. You are the one that has to live it every day.

Please, don't fall into the trap of thinking that your ex will be worse off if you do leave, because he wont. Just like you, he will get the lessons that he needed to learn and grow, just as you will.

Remember – relationships are about growth. And facing your fear is part of the letting go process.

Face the fear

I was once told the story of the North American buffalo that has to walk through the northern winds to get to his destination. Now the winds can be brutal, but the buffalo knows that if he takes the wind head on, that there is peace on the other side —that at some point the winds will stop and he will have arrived at his destination. You are on a similar journey and all I want to say is that it is time to walk through and confront, so that you can enjoy the fruits of your labour.

I know that it can take time to change and I know that it can be scary, but hang in there. It took me a good ten years to finally face my demons properly and look at what part I had to play in the relationships I had taken part in. Was it scary? Hell yes! Blimey, it was like standing on the precipice and deciding whether I was going to jump!

Did I want to look at my part? No, I didn't, and so for many years I would run away and keep repeating the same patterns of behaviour over and over. I would numb myself with drugs and alcohol and even have affairs—I would do anything to escape—anything and everything!

But I had no choice—well I did, but it didn't seem like I did. I still remember the day I found myself at the Beth Israel Hospital in New York City, waiting for a doctor to give me something to calm me down as I was ready to take my life that day. The pain I was feeling from the split from my ex-husband was so bad I honestly did not know how I was going to carry on. But I dragged myself there because I knew it would stop me from doing anything stupid.

As I sat there, I knew that I had hit rock bottom. I found myself sitting next to a drug addict who had been on a coke binge for the previous four days and was waiting to get the help he needed for his withdrawals. It was at this point that I thought to myself, *How the hell did I get here? How the hell did I attract a guy with a severe drug addiction?* I realized years on that he was just reflecting how I felt inside—which was empty.

This was only two weeks into my divorce. I had spent the previous couple of weeks chain smoking, numbing myself with alcohol and was on the verge of spending thousands of dollars on a psychic to get my ex back. My state was so bad that I even had homeless guys spitting at me, which had never happened before. I couldn't sleep and was so traumatized that after a heavy night of drinking, I peed on myself. I didn't wash for days and my tongue went black from all the cigarettes I smoked. I share this with you here frankly, in case you might think I couldn't possibly relate to how bad you might feel. Believe me, I can!

I found myself in the Big Apple—a strange, big city—without my security blanket—my ex-partner. I lost a stone in weight. I couldn't wash myself and every day was a living hell of pain. I just didn't care and it seemed that everybody around me, including my family, didn't either. I didn't think I could make it. I remember having to have strangers I met from the divorce group I had joined come and keep me company so I could fall asleep, only to wake up in the middle of night to realize that the nightmare I was living was real. I must have obsessed about whose fault it was for months, and I couldn't stop blaming myself for being the bad person I felt I must have been to have ended up in a failed marriage. In short, I felt like a failure.

... But I don't want that for you! I don't want you to get to that point. Maybe you already have, or hopefully you are in a much better place. Wherever you are at the moment, things don't have to carry on, which is why working beyond the resistance is really important for the change to happen.

However, what I learnt was that there are no such thing as failures—just situations that don't work out that will lead to new opportunities. I now know that I wasn't my failed marriage nor the relationship I had with my ex-husband. I was me with a past and a relationship that had challenges that I was not able to overcome or understand at the time. And the same is true for you—you are not a failure. You too are much more than a failed relationship.

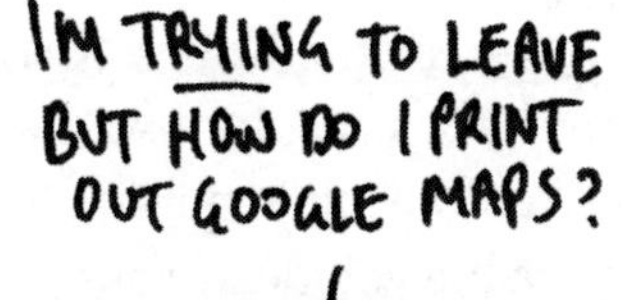

I see a lot of women who tell me that they don't have the resources to finance a coach, a workshop, or the books that can help them when they are clearly struggling. This way of thinking is exactly why they struggle and cannot move on. They limp into their next relationship with the same unpacked baggage and that stops them short from having the relationship they want, or the life they deserve.

The universe we live in is abundant and thinking you don't have the money to do what you want is a myth. *You can have anything you want right now by finding a way to get it.* The women I have seen rise into their greatness didn't necessarily have the money to change, but what they did have was the *commitment and courage* that allowed them to step into having a *much more resourceful mindset.*

Instead of saying, "I cannot afford it", they asked the question *"How can I afford it?"* They borrowed money off friends or family; sold items on eBay; did whatever it took to make the changes, as they knew that if *they* didn't change, nothing would. As a result, they got their return on their investment tenfold and more. What value can you place on having the life you desire and living it from a place of balance and power?

To overcome your fears and excuses, it is key to know your WHY—**Why you commit to letting go and move on..**

Without your WHY, your fears will cloud your dreams. Once you know your *why,* the *how's* will take care of themselves.

EXERCISE: Working out your WHY

Take a moment right now to get out a piece of paper and pen and **write down the *reasons for fully committing to letting go*** of the hurt, guilt, resentment, anger and fear.

Make sure that the WHY is big enough for you ... otherwise you may find yourself not motivated enough.

And then answer the following questions:

- What do I want in my life?
- If I knew that letting go would give me what I want, would there be any reason for me not to?

So now that you have committed and expressed how you feel, it's time for us to move onto releasing these emotions to feel the S.H.I.F.T.

PART 2: RELEASE

SEE YOUR REFLECTION IN YOUR EX

"The seen, the seeing and the seer are the same"

Nisargadatta Maharaj

The second step towards your freedom is to see your ex as a reflection of the parts of you that you judge—and you then extend that judgement to him.

Being in judgement of your ex, of yourself, or living in the fear of what others will think about what happened, will keep you stuck, resentful and stressed. Are you still judging him for hurting you? For not having picked up the kids on time, or for not caring? *After all that time we spent together, why does he just not seem to care?* Or are you judging yourself for not having done more, been more?

If you are in judgement or fear of it, this chapter will be invaluable to you. You see, if you keep judging him or punishing yourself, you won't ever get off the emotional rollercoaster and you will just keep on pointing the finger at him, which will keep you angry and hurt.

Judgement and its roots

Judgement usually comes from the unconscious wanting to be right. It creates a win/lose mentality. Do you remember in the last chapter I briefly mentioned that one of the main fears my clients go through which stops them from letting go is because they fear getting it wrong? Well this fear, manifests judgement.

If you are in a state of judgement, where you think only you are right, you will usually put him 'in the judgement pit'. In part, your response to him is, in a sense, saying "I would never do that." or "That is just wrong". But note you will only judge that which goes against the things you find important. And the viewpoint of 'I am right' makes you feel great. It makes you feel that you have the power.

What I want you to do right now is clench your fist and stamp your foot and say, "I am right." Didn't that feel amazing! Didn't it make you feel that you were somehow winning?—that somehow, if you were to let go of it that, you would lose? But this really is not the case.

The problem with this viewpoint is that it will keep you in judgement and you will struggle to let go, for fear that you will lose. The truth is that by putting yourself in that stance, your ex has already won. Holding onto these judgements will enable him to become a squatter in your head as he lives there rent-free.

If you don't let go of the judgement of what he has done and not done, then you will definitely find yourself struggling to move on.

So, where does the need to be right come from?

The sense of right and wrong would have come from your parents. When you were a little girl, your parents would have led you to believe that there were certain ways of being that were either right or wrong, based upon what they perceived to be right and wrong, based upon what their parents would have believed to be right or wrong, and so this goes on, from generation to generation.

As a child you were born with all aspects of your personality both 'bad' and 'good'. But what happens here is that your parents wanted to keep you safe. You then learnt to decipher what was right and wrong based upon the reaction that you got from your parents and others of influence in your life.

Disowned parts

THIS IS MY DISOWNED
SELF. SHE'S A BITCH

You were either rewarded for doing something right or reprimanded for doing something wrong. As being reprimanded for your behaviour would have become too painful, you then decided to just play safe and not exhibit that behaviour. At that point, you disowned it. You decided to just pretend you were no longer like that; you had been told being that way was not good, so you stopped.

If anybody shows up now with a part of you that you were reprimanded for having as a child, you judge them for it.

I have come to realize that the traits that I didn't like in my exes were *my disowned parts*. We have disowned and denied the parts of ourselves that we realised at a young age were 'not supposed to be expressed', based upon the expectations of our parents, teachers, or other influences in our life at that time.

The example that illustrates this point better than anything else that I have seen is one of the opening scenes in the *Prince of Tides* where Nick Nolte and his wife, on the verge of divorce, are walking along the beach. She wants to talk to him about their issues, but he just keeps turning her concerns into jokes. She then complains that she feels pushed away by his reaction, but he denies it and tells her that she takes everything too seriously!

You later find out that when he was young, he was raped by intruders, as were the rest of his family. His mother decides that they should keep it a secret and that they shouldn't share what happened. Nick Nolte's way of dealing with it was to use his sense of humour to cope, so he shut himself off from his emotions as they appeared to be too painful to deal with. He then falls in love with somebody who expresses herself fully to him and awakens that part of himself that he has disowned.

That is why true self-acceptance can be so challenging. If you have been programmed all your life to think that you're supposed to be a certain way and that some part of you is wrong, then how can you ever accept *others* for who *they* really are? This might be the very reason why you may be finding it challenging to accept something about your ex that you think is wrong.

What happened to your other half?

"Find the strength to love that part of yourself you hate in the other person, to break down the barriers of attrition and resistance." ~ Marina Pearson

You picked your ex based upon your subconscious search to find the disowned parts of you, to make you feel whole.

But on first going out with him and falling in love, the parts that you found so complementary were the parts that you admired about him, right? It's like you somehow managed to fit all the jigsaw pieces together perfectly. What a wonderful combination it was—until it was not.

Research shows that when you're falling in love, your dopamine levels skyrocket and your oxytocin levels soar! These are feel-good chemicals that are released in the body as a response to the person you are falling in love with. I liken this experience to taking hallucinogenic drugs. You're exposed to life being more colourful and your awareness is heightened.

Any time your ex judges you for something, just remember he is judging that part of himself he was told not to be.

Just like a junky who needs a fix, you end up wanting to be fixed by them 24/7. Every time you see them your heart races, your world lights up, everything has sharpness and a colour to it that you hadn't quite noticed before. Colours are more vivid; they swirl and dance around you. Time stops, but your sexual appetite doesn't! Nobody has been as caring, as loving, and as wonderful as they have. You may even hear yourself saying—"Wow, they are the same as me!"

Falling in love is just an infatuation with a fantasy. You only see what you want to see, and project what you see onto them. This is just an illusion as your perception is what you choose to see, justified by your belief filters, as discussed previously.

You live with this until one day they change. You think to yourself, *What happened? Where did my original honey bunny go?* The answer is "Nowhere". They were always there; you were just blind to the downsides as you chose not to see them as a direct result of your dopamine fix.

These disowned parts then become an issue. They press your buttons. You get angry or frustrated at something that they do, such as being late, or that they lie, or are arrogant, or they will not let you speak to the kids. You start to think that they are wrong for being that way and you begin to judge them for being like that. This in turn can bring on the arguments and disagreements, exacerbating your feelings of anger, resentment and hurt.

What if he is judging me? If he is judging you for something—get excited! It's an opportunity for you to learn about yourself. If he is judging you for being too needy, too pushy, or too crazy, understand that he will be judging that in himself.

CASE STUDY: Leila's story

I was working with Leila and she started judging herself because her ex was judging her for being too pushy, too crazy, and so on. So I decided to describe him. I described him as very independent, not overtly emotional, serious with a bit of a stiff upper lip. She looked at me incredulously and asked, "How did you know that?" and I answered. "Whatever he is judging you for is that which he perceives himself not to be."

A big light bulb went on for her as she realized that she was just expressing the bits of him he had disowned. The moment she could see this, her resentment for herself dissolved and she felt at peace. *So any time your ex judges you for something, just remember he is judging that part of himself he was told not to be.*

EXERCISE: Repeat after me:

"There is nothing wrong with me, I am perfect as I am; he is judging me for something that he wishes he wasn't."

The truth is we are all one

"There is nothing we can see or conceive that we are not, and the purpose of the journey is to restore ourselves to our wholeness." ~ Debbie Ford

This quote by Debbie Ford, author of the *Dark Side of Light Chasers,* has stuck with me ever since I read it. It is in sync with a new theory that the universe is based upon a holographic model. According to this theory, every piece of the universe, no matter how we slice it off, contains *the intelligence of the whole*. Just like a hologram, if you cut it up and look only at any one small piece of it, you can still see the *whole of the image*.

Now I know this may sound a little bit 'woo-woo' to some, but if you think about it, it makes complete sense. This model provides us with a completely new paradigm of looking at things, of seeing the connection between our inner and outer world.

According to Deepak Chopra "***we are not in the world, but the world is in us***." We are the microcosm within the macrocosm, just like in the universe where there is both dark and light. This means that you and I have every trait known to man within us. We are both a saint and a sinner, both selfish and unselfish. For more information, read Gregg Braden's book, *The Divine Matrix.* It will give you a completely different perspective on the world you live in and how it works.

What will work – Embrace what you judge!

"Turn your wounds into wisdom." **~ Oprah Winfrey**

By turning your wounds into wisdom, you will finally be able to let go of the pain you feel around what you judge in him and in his judgement of you. By embracing those parts of *yourself* that you judge in him, you will also be able to embrace those parts of you that have been crying out all along to be embraced.

And here's some more good news: As you embrace the parts of *him* that push your buttons, you will be better able to embrace the nice parts of you too!

You cannot truly embrace what is nice about you without recognising and embracing your dark bits too. They go hand in hand. If you resist embracing that part of you that you push away in your ex, it will keep persisting. As the famous saying goes, "What you resist persists!" We are just like magnets. If you are negatively charged about a particular type of aspect within people (a disowned part of yourself), you *will* attract a person who expresses that aspect and does so without having a problem with it. The only way to dissolve your negative charge so that you don't keep attracting it into your life is by turning it into positive one.

As mentioned before, your ex is just a mirror to you. The more you embrace your dark parts, the more you will be able to embrace those of your ex, and things will change. A hero cannot exist without his archenemy. Luke Skywalker would have had no reason to be if Darth Vader had not existed.

An aspect is just an aspect, *until you judge it*. Have you ever had to be selfish to save your own skin? Have you ever had to be mean to protect yourself? These traits that you may judge *have value. Everything serves.* I had a client who judged her ex for being selfish, but when she realized that her own selfishness had actually saved her life—because it meant she left an abusive relationship—she shifted the way she saw selfishness. *Sometimes you have to be a certain way to honour who you are.*

Another aspect my clients often judge within their ex is his lying. If you see lying as bad, this will upset you. But have you ever been in a situation where you felt you had to lie to save somebody else's feelings? People don't tell the truth because of their own fears and because they may want to protect others. If you can see how that aspect of your ex serves you and how your being that way does the same, there is no need to judge it anymore.

Remember: Use the mantra—A trait is just a trait until I judge it!

My disowned part story

THIS IS MY DISOWNED
SELF. SHE'S A BITCH

As with most things I share in this book, I have **experienced this first-hand and have seen countless of examples with others where** this is true. As I have already mentioned, one of my biggest challenges was confrontation. As a child, expressing what I truly thought was deemed 'bad'. Even when I was angry or upset, I would hide what I felt and deal with it on my own.

Being a girl, being nice and polite were always going to be on the top of the list. So much so, that I ended up with a people-pleasing pattern, which in the end was to the detriment of my own health and well-being and manifested in my anorexia, drug taking and alcohol abuse. I would do anything to fit in. This mainly came in the guise of pleasing men sexually and doing things they wanted, not what I wanted; hanging out with people I thought were friends but who turned out to be party acquaintances at best. The more I attempted to be one-sided, the more depressed and lost I became.

In fact, forcing myself to be kind, nice and polite, among many other perceived positive traits, was energy sapping. Over the years, this put a lot of stress on my body. My hair started to fall out and I became really tired. In short, my attempt to hide the bad bits of me over the years finally took its toll when I went for a check-up and found out that I was completely depleted of all the minerals and vitamins that I needed to function properly. If I had carried on the way I was going, I would have ended up on the road of no return.

I judged myself for being a fake; but worse still were the judgements on myself for the things that were deemed bad. Whenever I had an argument with any of my exes, I would judge myself as a bad person. Whenever I didn't say thank you to somebody, I would judge myself for not having done so. I lived a life of guilt and shame, perceiving myself as bad and, of course, I would also act on this belief.

The great thing is that once you know what you judge your ex for, you can then begin to explore what you judge in yourself. It is always worth remembering that when you point the finger at him, you have three fingers pointing back at you.

SUCH LOVELY NAILS, TOO

I know no other way to fully find peace with your ex than by you finding peace with yourself. Facing your perceived darkness has to be part of this process. By doing this, you will be able to shift your perception and free yourself of your current frustrations.

It was not until I came across the work that I now use primarily with my clients that I could really begin to embrace who I was in my totality. The rewards of the work are enormous, and so they have been for my clients.

I do want you to remember though, that a *perceived* bad trait *is not necessarily a bad trait. It's both good and bad.* It all depends on how you have been brought up and the angle from which you are looking at it.

Learning to love my confrontational side through George

George is an ex of mine who I went out with after my divorce and I used to find him very confrontational. When we first met, I did not see this side of him—actually I *did not want* to see this side of him. I could only see more upsides than downsides, so my perceptions of him were definitely not in balance. However, all that ended when he started to confront me and say things and do things to me that, in my mind, were mean.

I remember one time when I slipped on a piece of ice and fell over. Rather than coming over to pick me up, he turned around, saw that I was on the ground hurting, then laughed and walked away. To make matters worse at that time, he got angry because I was angry with him. In my naivety I thought that getting angry would help! I was so angry with him because in my mind I wanted him to come and pick me up and tell me everything was going to be okay. I judged him for his meanness and for always wanting to be confrontational. Of course, these were parts of me that I was denying and perceived that I couldn't, or didn't want to, express.

As a young child I learnt that to express myself fully was dangerous. Because of this, I would hide away from confrontation. So of course, (in retrospect) it was an obvious gift for me to have somebody like George show up to get me to find and love that part of me.

George was also the catalyst for me to finally embrace the beauty of speaking my truth. By embracing these parts of myself, I was able to express my thoughts openly, which as a speaker is really important! I thank him every day for having taught me to stand up for myself and to speak my truth.

What I learnt was that once you own those bits you don't like about your ex, those bits about him *won't own you* anymore. Those particular behaviours of his that you don't like will not *bother you anymore*. You free yourself of them. This happened to me with George. After doing the process of embracing the aspects within him that I did not like, he softened and no longer used his anger as a weapon. I also freed myself of the fear and I felt more at peace.

The question is how do you dissolve the judgement towards yourself and your ex, so that you start to free yourself of the anger and hurt? Well the good news is that you can kill two birds with one stone and dissolve the judgements you feel towards him and yourself at the same time!

By doing the following exercise that I have used in my *Goodbye Mr Ex,* workshop you will be able to start doing just that.

EXERCISE: Little Miss Exercise

Step 1: Write down the aspect of your ex that you judge him for e.g. selfish

Step 2: Write down at least 5 people who may have seen you express this trait or where you could possibly conceive yourself being this way if the situation arose where you had to be so.

Step 3: Draw that part of you into a character and call her your Little Miss..... (In this case you would name her *Little Miss Selfish*)

Step 4: Take a moment to sit and close your eyes and imagine that she is standing there in front of you and ask her

What positive qualities does she bring you and others around you?

- What gifts does she bring you?
- How does she serve you?
- What does she want you to pay attention to?
- How can you both get along now?

To get the full guided visualisation for this exercise go to www.GoodbyeMrEx.com/LittleMiss.

You can now do this exercise with whatever you judge him for, which will start to make you feel lighter as a result.

PART I

HEAL YOUR CONSCIOUS STORY

"The world is nothing but my perception of it. I see only through myself. I hear only through the filter of my story."

Byron Katie

So by now you may have realized that you have a 'story' about your ex—about what he has done or not done, about how he has hurt you or pushed your buttons. All the story does is keep you enslaved to him, while you become the victim of your own story. The problem is that questioning it all, over and over again, rehashing what has happened, will just keep you stuck.

In truth, you have *two* stories. You will have a conscious one and an unconscious one. A story of the here and now and another one *that you are not even aware of.* The former is what I will be talking about in this chapter and I will address the latter after that.

The longer you keep this going, the longer your 'inner hamster' will keep on going around and around and around the victim wheel—keeping you prisoner and allowing your ex to live rent free in your head, controlling you.

Stories and perceptions

A story is an interpretation of facts that you then add meaning to. Let me give you an example:

He left (is a fact). Why he left (is the meaning you give to it).

He hasn't picked up the kids (is a fact). Why he hasn't (is the meaning you give to it).

What the story comes down to is based on a perception of what you see.

Perception is really *the meaning* you give to something. It's *your take* on things. Perception is your sensory experience of the world around you and involves both the recognition of environmental stimuli and your actions in response to these stimuli. In other words, it is how you make sense of the world around you. Not everybody experiences the world around them in the same way. Your perception will be determined by your education, how you were brought up, your belief systems and values, and other determinants.

Imagine a construction worker, a farmer and a botanist looking at a piece of land that includes a beautiful field with flowers. Do you think they will look at the scene in the same way, or will each of them see a different field based upon their point of view?

The construction worker might see the field and think the piece of land would be brilliant to build on. The farmer might wonder if the land has fertile soil to grow new vegetation. And finally, the botanist might get excited at the prospect of finding some exotic flower there. Each of these three individuals will have their own requirements and needs. They each see their world through very different glasses, as do you.

As human beings, we are 'meaning-making' machines. This means that you will make up your mind about whether something is good or bad based upon your beliefs and what you deem important to you.

You will tend to see things as *you are*, not as they are. Regarding your ex, you will be seeing him as you are, not as he truly is. I have always said that there are four people living in each relationship:

1. You
2. The perception your ex has of you
3. Your ex
4. The perception that you have of your ex

Do you find yourself dancing between the memories of the bad times and the good, while cursing him for his behavior one moment and thinking that nobody will ever be as amazing as him, the next? The challenge with going backwards and forwards between these opposing unbalanced perceptions is that they will render you powerless and keep you hostage to the Victim Cycle.

The Victim Cycle

The Victim Cycle looks something like this:

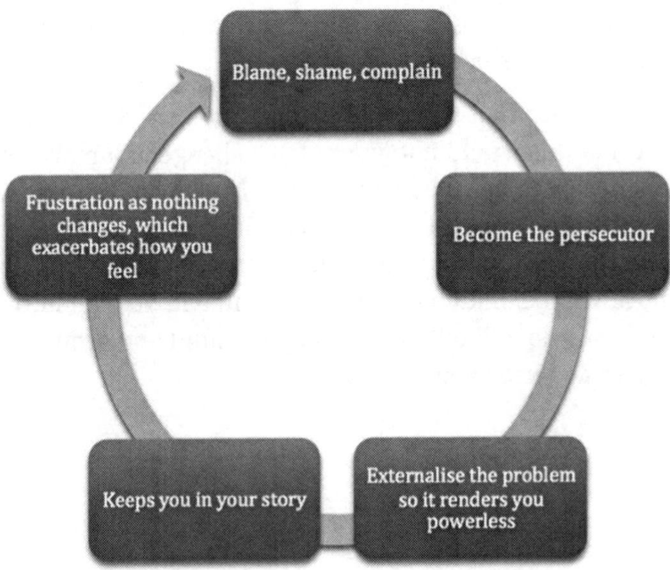

The problem with being on the Victim Cycle is that you are caught up in a loop that feeds itself with the guarantee that your ex will have you hooked forever unless you choose to break away from it and do something about it.

If you find yourself *at effect* (meaning that things happen to you) versus *at the cause* (meaning that you take responsibility) then you give your power away to your ex, as you can do nothing about it.

I recently had a lady come to me who couldn't understand why her ex had changed his mind about her; why he didn't want to be in a relationship with her anymore. She kept telling me that she was the sort of person who would fight for what she wanted. She thought that if she behaved in a certain way that she would get the outcome that she was looking for.

I told her that she could behave any way she wanted, but that this would not guarantee a change in him. When you decide to behave in a certain way with an outcome in mind, it won't work. It's like a game of chess. You can select your move, thinking you know what your opponent's move will be, but you cannot guarantee it. Staying in the Victim Cycle will only have you go around and around in circles and keep you obsessing.

The Tractor Factor

Have you realized now that by staying in this cycle, nothing actually changes? You just end up becoming more frustrated because you feel stuck. By rehashing the story, you are just carving a deeper and deeper groove into your negative thought pattern. I call this the 'Tractor Factor'. Imagine your thoughts are like a tractor, ploughing the same field in the same place over and over and over. What happens? The groove gets deeper, doesn't it? This is what happens with your thought pattern; it gets more and more ingrained, until that becomes your story.

Holding onto your feelings of anger is like drinking

poison and expecting the other person to die. *The only person it really affects is you.*

If you find yourself saying things like "He did this to me" and "Because he did that, I now feel this way..." you know that you are on the *effect* side of the equation.

Take healthy self-responsibility

***"You must take personal responsibility. You cannot change the circumstances, the seasons, or the wind, but you can change yourself. That is something you have charge of."* ~ Jim Rohn**

I have already expressed this to some degree, yet I want to make the point again and in more depth. *Healthy self-responsibility is very important if you want to re-claim your power and move forward.* It's easy when you know how.

Healthy self-responsibility is the ability to look at yourself and understand what part you play in the dynamic that you currently have with your ex. This is the ability to be at the *cause* side of the equation. This is not about beating yourself up or anything like that; it's about ensuring you don't keep feeding your ex with your powerlessness, which arises from externalizing the problem and creating your story around it. You will not learn by doing this; you certainly will not be able to move on and the anger will stick with you.

Move into the Empowerment Cycle

By shifting from the Victim Cycle into the Empowerment Cycle, you are making the bold statement that you are indeed the 'hostess with the mostess' and the mistress of your own destiny. Now I know this can seem super scary, but the good news is that *you can* start to change how you feel!

This is what the Empowerment Cycle looks like:

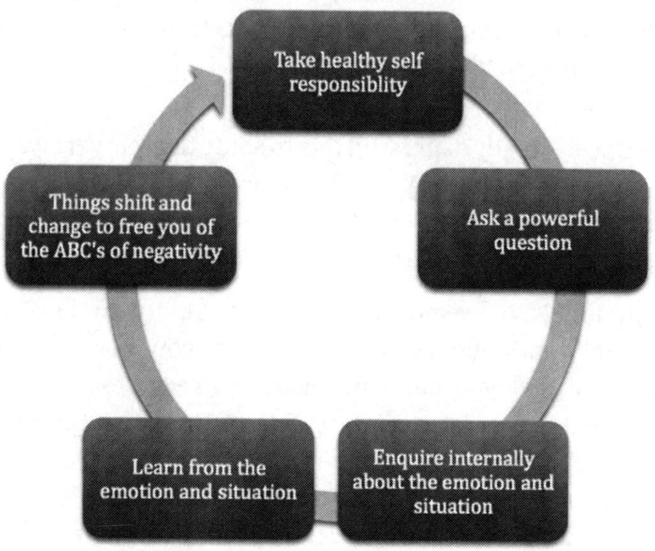

Let me give you an example.

Let's say the situation is that your ex has once again changed his plans. If you were coming from the Victim Cycle, you would probably get annoyed, frustrated and angry—which is completely valid by the way—but from the perspective of the Empowerment Cycle, you would ask yourself a question like:

"Where am I not taking 100 per cent self-responsibility for my part?"

This could mean that you are making it easy on him to change his plans. The emotions here could be anger and resentment, so when you inquire inside you might find, for instance, that the anger and resentment are actually more about you being angry at yourself for *letting* him treat you this way.

By this point you have learnt from the emotion and situation, so when it comes up again, you can *shift the way you do things* so that you don't get the same response. By being able to learn from what has just happened, you will stop going into your old story, so you can create a new one. By giving your story a new interpretation and giving it a shiny new meaning, you will feel better and see that your old story was just that—an old story.

Living in the Empowerment Cycle is fun

You may have the belief that change is hard and that it will open up a can of worms. But the truth is that your can of worms has already been opened. Are you not feeling stressed out and wishing you could get off the emotional rollercoaster? I often see women who resist the change and resist their healing. But it's actually just as painful for them to stay where they are as it would be to shift into the Empowerment Cycle and live from this new mindset. Yes, there are growing pains, but are there not pains now, anyway?

The women I know who have recovered from divorces and their break-ups by doing the work are the ones that are now living their dream life with their dream partner, in their dream house, doing their dream job and having the time of their life. Does it mean that there are never going to be any problems again? Of course not. Life will always throw challenges at you, but it *does mean they are able to cope with bigger challenges.*

Their comfort zone has expanded and keeps on doing so, so they are guaranteed to empower themselves in all areas of their life. And remember that life starts beyond your comfort zone and because of this they are full of vitality and doing what they love as a result. They are fully embracing life, with all its ups and downs, but they are doing so in a way that comes more naturally to them, as opposed to what it was like before, which was HARD.

Living here is fun for them! They get to meet some awesome people and they get to empower their family as a result. Their children (if they have them) benefit as they are being taught to see life through different eyes. As a result, their children have more opportunities and they get to grow up with an empowered mindset. How does it get any better than that?

They also finally have the financial resources that previously they had depended on their ex so much for. This, of course, is a huge step for any woman who wants to be independent and financially free. But this starts from being in a place of balance.

Balance

It is important to have a balanced perception in order to dissolve the emotion in your story. Emotions are lopsided perceptions—they are half-truths of a whole story. If you are able to see *both sides* of your own story, this will free you of the negative emotions you feel such as anger, guilt, sadness or even jealousy. Each emotion holds a story that is only half the truth. In life you cannot have a plus without a minus. There are always two sides of the coin. What goes up must come down; there is no darkness without light, no night without day. Yes, many clichés, but oh so true.

So why wouldn't there be two sides to *your* story?

If you are able to balance out a negative perception with a positive one, and a positive one with a negative, the emotion (whichever that may be) will dissolve and calmness will take its place. Your ex will also stop living rent free in your head as you will start to see him as he truly is, not just *as you see him*. But this is up to you. You have a *choice* to let go of your past and your hurt.

I want you to imagine your emotions like a see-saw. Just like a see-saw, you can come to a place of balance by seeing the good in the bad, and the bad in the good. It is in this moment that your yo-yo emotions disappear. It is at this place of balance, where you feel calm and quiet, that you can even access acceptance and then gratitude.

I often hear the expression that 'time is a healer', but I disagree. Time is only a healer if you are ready to let go and *use the time to heal*. It's what you do with your time that counts.

Remember I told you about George, my ex who taught me to embrace my own anger? Well it took me, ten years to finally let him go. I met him when I was nineteen years old and even throughout my marriage and after, I always kept one door open for him. It wasn't until we decided to commit to a serious relationship after my divorce that I realized that I had been living a fantasy of what being in a truly committed relationship with him would entail. A year later, we broke up and I finally made the decision to let him go. I always kept a candle burning for him, no matter what relationship I was in, which kept me in my own prison and fantasy story. What I learnt was that for me to be present in the relationship I was in, I would have to let go of the past.

This pattern of mine also played out with my ex-husband. Unbeknown to me (but obvious to a very good healer and friend of mine), I was still holding onto my ex-husband—even six years after the divorce. Even though I had not heard from him for that amount of time, I would still yearn for the relationship that we had—well the good things of course.

So I sent him an email to find out how he was. And I didn't hear back. Three months later, he replied to tell me that he was getting married and told me all the details of who she was and how lucky they were to be together. I found myself in complete shock! I knew this day had to come, but it hurt all the same. It brought up all of these old emotions that took me right back to when we got divorced.

What was really fascinating was that as I opened up the email, my flatmate's girlfriend was practising a presentation in the living room next door and I heard her talking about emotional triggers. The example she used was of hearing from an ex that you had not heard from in a while. It was as if she was talking about me!

Synchronicity! The message was clear.

I allowed my heart to fill with gratitude and wrote back and congratulated him on his news. What then came back was something quite extraordinary—a beautiful letter thanking me for being who I was and that he was touched that we had connected and that I had sent him my kind words.

I then decided right there and then I would let go, and I asked my friend the healer to release the sadness that I felt around having lost the relationship. After the session, a friend of mine who was pulling my heartstrings at the time, connected with me on Skype to ask how I was. Now this was strange, as he had not made contact with me since I had seen him two weeks before. He had also made it difficult for me to get in touch with him as "he was too busy to talk". I knew I was seeing him two days later and thought I would see how things unfolded.

Soon after, we got together and the rest is history—as this man is now my fiancé—and I now can see how right he is for me. Finally letting go of my ex-husband and George, I was able to finally attract the man that I could build my life with. I tell you this story to let you know *that this can happen to you if you put the work in.*

YOUR LIVING BLUEPRINT
Find Out What is Important To You

As I mentioned briefly before, your story will be made negative or positive based upon what you judge or find amazing about him, which will stem from your Living Blueprint. I am sure you are wondering 'What is my Living Blueprint?'

Your Living Blueprint is comprised of a list of factors that are important to you. These important factors are what you base your decisions on and they will dictate where you end up.

For example, some important factors in your life may be your career, learning, your health, or your family. You might prioritise between these factors—your work or your family may come first, and something like learning might come after that—but nobody has to get you up in the morning to do any of these things, as you *love doing them.*

No two people on the planet have the same Living Blueprint. This blueprint is completely unique to you, just as it will be unique to your ex. When the important factors of your Living Blueprint are challenged or compromised in a relationship, you will naturally move away from that person. But when you engage with somebody who has a similar Living Blueprint to you, you will feel connected and be more inclined to like them.

I can now see that conflict and being upset comes because either one of the two people, or both, want the other to be more like them and change their blueprint to suit them. This can be defined as an *uncaring relationship.*

The uncaring relationship

Projecting what you deem important onto your ex will only exacerbate your anger and resentment and will not achieve anything. Your ex will have his own Living Blueprint. The mistake I see most women make is that *they assume that their ex values the same things as they do.* To expect your ex to be more like you and to find important what you find important will NOT work! When you find that he is not like you, this makes you angry and will spin the wheels of resentment and hurt faster and faster.

Let me give you an example: A client was stressed and upset about the fact that her ex didn't seem to care about their child, as he was not paying (in her perception) his fair share for his children's support. She was so annoyed that she took him to court and won. Now, I am sure that reading this you can relate to her, right? Well, at first glance, as a mum, of course you would get upset and angry at the fact that your ex is not paying up.

What I got from this story, however, was that although he did have children and did have a family, his values did not lie in his family. He loved to work, make money, live a bachelor's lifestyle and drive fast cars. Yes, he had taken his kids on holiday, but he definitely does not act, in her eyes, as a supportive dad would.

There is no right or wrong here, just a different person, doing his own thing. You may argue that if he didn't want kids, then he shouldn't have had them. But as you now know, there is never a negative without a positive, or a positive without a negative. His kids will benefit just as much from him being the way he is, as they won't.

As you can start to see, your story of what your ex has done or not done will be based upon what he finds important in his life, and if it differs from your perception of what is important without you knowing about this, then you will feel that he neither cares nor respects who you are.

Just as you may find yourself in an uncaring relationship, you might yourself in a cautious one.

The cautious relationship

I find that most of the women that come to me were actually living in a cautious relationship before their break-up. Most had *compromised who they were* and therefore spent most of their time walking on eggshells, just to please their partner.

Was it something that served them? Of course it was. It allowed them to keep the peace; but did it allow them to be truly who they are? No. It may well be that they compromised their career, or that they took on the role of being a mother when all they wanted was to carry on with their career. Do you think they will have a negative story about this? Sure they will, as their Living Blueprint has been compromised.

If at any point you hear yourself saying that is something that I HAVE TO DO, I MUST DO or SHOULD DO then these are not going to be what is actually important to you. When you hear yourself saying these words, you know that you have subjected yourself to somebody else's Living Blueprint. The problem with this is that you are not only 'should-ing', 'have-ing' and 'must-ing' yourself, but you are also minimizing yourself to others' way of living—acting like theirs is the best way for you, when in reality it is not.

The 'others' usually include your parents, society, culture, your peers, your ex, your environment or school. In short, any outside influence can have a huge impact on whether you perceive that something is your value or somebody else's.

I know this one very well. I come from a Spanish family and for them family is a very important component of what they deem important. My family value their family, but for the most part I find my relationship to my fiancé, friends and my business at the heart of my life.

This has definitely been an issue in the past, as close family members did not like the fact that I would focus on my friendships rather than wanting to spend time with them. I suppose I didn't really ever perceive my family to be missing out on my presence and, instead, friends were more important to me. As I had a pattern that revolved around wanting to please those around me, I would do what was expected of me by my family, instead of what I really wanted to do. This caused me a lot of stress and this will do the same for you if you carry on without recognising your differences.

The thoughtful relationship

So what constitutes a *thoughtful relationship*? This is when two people respect the other person for who they are and don't want to change them to how they want them to be. Anything else is a selfish act. WE are all DIFFERENT! If you don't get anything else from this book other than this, then you are well on the way to mastering your next relationship and understanding your situation with your ex.

Creating a thoughtful relationship for you with your ex is about getting to know what his Living Blueprint is and how the important factors in either of your blueprints can help you both get what you want.

For example, it may well be he is fulfilled by learning, whereas your career might be what is important to you. Well, how can his love for learning help you with your career? If you start with that one question then your perception and story around *'how he spent most of his time doing what you didn't want him to do, while you slaved your guts out'*, will shift and allow you to see him being truly who he is. Do we not just want to be loved for who we are?

To find your Living Blueprint you can download the questions from www.GoodbyeMrEx.com/LivingBluePrint.

CASE STUDY:
Jen's Story – From cautious to thoughtful

I recently worked with a couple—Malcolm and Jen—who were struggling to overcome their frustrations and resentments towards Malcolm's ex-wife (Valery). Firstly, Jen was struggling with her behaviour in general. Both Jen and Malcolm had to move from Manchester to Glasgow as the ex-wife decided to move to the North of Scotland with his daughter. For many months before, they had to endure a 14 hour round trip from Manchester to pick up his daughter, only to repeat it a few days later to take her back.

The ex, Valery, had promised to share some of the travel, but changed her plans as soon as she arrived in Scotland and only made the journey to Manchester twice. Does this sound familiar? Have you had this sort of thing happen to you?

As a result, Malcolm and Jen both decided to leave Manchester and settle in Glasgow, several hundred miles from Jen's family. This also bothered her. As if the lying, moving and travelling was not enough, Valery was also impolite and would put Malcolm and Jen down right in front of them and this was now rubbing off on Malcolm and Valery's child.

When I met to work with them, it was clear that Jen was struggling to accept Valery and the situation they both found themselves in. She was upset and angry, not only at Valery but at Malcolm too for not understanding how she felt. In addition, she could not understand why Malcolm was taking it all in his stride and she would get frustrated by his not 'standing up' to his ex.

I realized that he had in fact finally come to terms with the situation and that he had been working hard to disentangle himself from Valery. Malcolm had gotten used to the dynamic and had picked up strategies in the course of their relationship that equipped him to deal with her. He would simply let the majority of her behaviour wash over him.

As the person who had instigated the break up with Valery, Malcolm had already had time to make peace with Valery and the overall situation as it unfolded, whereas Jen was just catching up with it all. Malcolm would naturally have had time to think about his relationship with his ex long ago, look at it from different angles and finally, in this new situation, to respond more calmly to Valery and ultimately accept the decision to move to Scotland.

By taking Jen through the process, I was able to help her *shift her way of thinking toward her situation* and see *the truth of what was going on* and see that Valery *was* not the nightmare that she thought she was, *nor was there only one way to see her.*

The story she had chosen to tell herself was one of woe and anger. By answering a set of questions by me, her story changed. Now she was able to see the blessings behind the lying and the move; behind the travel; behind Val's being so impolite.

Jen discovered the move to Glasgow, brought on by Valery's move, actually meant that Malcolm's working hours had changed for the better. He now only worked four days a week, rather than the six he was working in Manchester.

This meant that they had more time to spend together. He had time to concentrate on his creativity and she did too. In fact, her frustration had sent her into the most creative space that she had to date experienced. As she had time on her hands, she found that she would spend it more with her artwork and less working, which she wanted to move away from as she was already two months' pregnant.

Jen was in a moment of transition. They had found a lovely house, which she could embrace fully. It was quiet, near the shops and had amazing energy, with the advantage that the walls were empty, giving her opportunity to paint big and bold to fill up the space. At that point, she was even contemplating setting herself up as an artist. Her paintings were amazing and served as therapy for her, calming her, not to mention what it would be doing for the baby. Being in Glasgow certainly *was* now ticking her boxes, especially the ones of her highest values. She had just needed some help seeing that.

Now there was still an obstacle to get over. The 4-hour journey they still needed to do to collect Malcolm's daughter. Jen was still frustrated that they were the ones to do this. However, what she now started seeing was that she and Malcolm could spend more time together, get creative and travel to different places on the way to discover parts of Scotland they had not seen before.

Now that they had discovered an unearthed passion for travel, they were thinking of buying a camper van so that they could live the simple life that they so much enjoyed. They also noticed that the quality of life had improved in Scotland. You can definitely get more for your buck there and the work/life balance is much more conducive to a less stressful life, especially for Malcolm who works for the NHS. Granted, the weather is not all that great, but it meant that they could focus more on making the inside of their house a home.

They also discovered that they actually had more independence from Valery. There was Jen thinking that they were under Valery's thumb, but they actually now had more freedom than they did when they were all in Manchester, as the distance had been shortened and they were able to set up their life as they wished without much discussion from the opponent. They were planning to buy a house in the next twelve months and would be free to choose anywhere that Malcolm could commute from. As Valerie no longer lived around the corner, she would have no influence on this decision.

Finally, the last point was that Jen was still annoyed that her parents were so far away. However, she once again moved past seeing the drawbacks to seeing the benefits to her and her partner. This way, her parents could in fact spend *more quality time* when they visited. Just as her parents could do this, she realized that *her friends could do this too.* They had had more visitors in three months in Glasgow than in a year in Manchester. They also now had the house that was big enough to invite more people and look after them too.

What was amazing, that I certainly was not expecting, was that as they worked through her fears and frustrations, they dealt with one of their biggest blocks, which they had not even known was there. Jen felt that Malcolm had not expressed why he had loved Valery. He admitted it had been out of convenience.

Then Jen felt Malcolm wanted to paint a very different picture for his daughter. Jen was very upset as she felt so left out, as without the full picture of his past, she couldn't work out what was true. He had not realized that she wanted to look at photos of them when they were happy, as he thought they would upset her. However, he found out that this in fact was not true and it was his *not sharing* them with her that was upsetting her even more, as she had a very skewed view of who he portrayed Valery to be.

It was at this point that the block shifted and they were able to talk through the information she needed from him, which he was happy to share.

The other thing that Jen was very much upset about was the fact that Valery tended to be impolite and she found her quite rude. However, we explored how it would have been if Valery had been the polite and sweet person she wished she would be and found that if she had, Malcolm would probably still be confused as to whether or not he had made the right decision. It was this trait, as well as a few others, that had made him leave in the first place. She realized that the ruder Valery had got, the closer she and Malcolm had become. In essence Valery's rudeness had drawn them closer.

I challenged Jen and asked her whether she would have liked Valery to have been calling up and being lovely all the time? Whether this would have made her more confused too about how Malcolm felt and whether this might have brought about jealousy instead of the resentment? She acknowledged that it would have done. At this point, she realized *that neither way was better or worse*. It would have just been a *different scenario*.

Because of the issues with Valerie, they had to be sure to keep their communication channels wide open, so they became very good at communicating with one another. They also realized that the testing times had indeed made their relationship stronger and had given them a much more in-depth understanding of one another—one that they probably would not have had if they had not had to confront something as challenging as the ex-wife.

Jen had bought books on being a step-mum and she and Malcolm had worked through Malcolm's thoughts and feelings about the situation. In short, they realized that Malcolm's ex was highlighting that their relationship would stand the test of time and had given them a number of tools and skills that had made them come to the realization that they were supposed to be together.

Finally, they also realized how their behaviour had contributed to Valery's perceived challenging personality too. They had wanted to include her in their dynamic—there was even talk of going for meals together. It was obvious by talking to them that Valery was in no position to take this on and wanted to be left alone.

Also Valery did not want to travel, nor did she feel it important to be polite around them. She obviously did not value travel or politeness. Remember, any aspect—what is important to another—that you might judge of another is *neutral until you judge it.*

In short, there is never a drawback without a benefit. *Seeing both sides* of your story will open you up to the truth of your ex and release you from the frustration and resentment that you feel.

Let's have a go at re-writing your story with your ex.

Re-writing your 'ex' story

EXERCISE:

Just like Jen, you can change your story!

Create 5 sentences to define your 'ex' story. Write down 5 things he did and assign to them the negative meaning you gave to them or still give to them. For example, the first might be that *'my ex left, which means that he is mean and selfish'*.

The OLD story is:

1. My ex ______________________________ ______________ which means that ______________ ____ ____.

2. He then ______________________________ ______________ which means that ______________ ____ ____.

3. My ex ______________________________ ______________ which means that ______________ ____ ____.

4. He then ______________________________ ______________ which means that ______________ ____ ____.

5. My ex______________________________
____________ which means that ______________
____
____.

Now you can give positive meanings to the same action. For example, 'My ex left, which means that I have more time for myself and I can meet new people while I learn and grow.'

Write down 3 new, positive meanings for each negative thing he did that you listed above.

The NEW story is:

1. My ex ______________________________
__________which means that

- ______________________________________
____
- ______________________________________
____
- ______________________________________
____

2. He then ____________________________
____________ which means that

- ______________________________________
____
- ______________________________________
____
- ______________________________________
____

3. He then ______________________________
______________ which means that

- ______________________________
____
- ______________________________
____
- ______________________________
____

4. He then ______________________________
______________ which means that

- ______________________________
____
- ______________________________
____
- ______________________________
____

5. He then ______________________________
______________ which means that

- ______________________________
____
- ______________________________
____
- ______________________________
____

How do you feel now that you have read your new story? Keep reading it every day until the new way of seeing your situation sinks in. You can always add more to your new story if you wish.

Well, just as there is a conscious story, which we have just discussed, there is also an unconscious story. So, let's move onto *Chapter 4 Part 2: Healing Your Unconscious Story.*

PART 2

HEAL YOUR UNCONSCIOUS STORY

"Our task is to become conscious of the contents that press upwards from the unconscious."

Carl Jung

Until now we have been working on seeing the other side to your conscious story. However, there is also an unconscious story—the story of your childhood past that you are probably not consciously aware of.

Whenever you have your buttons pushed by your ex, whether it was at the time of your break-up or now, remember—your ex is not the source of your pain, *he is just the trigger of it.* Your ex is just shining a light on a wound that was formed when you were very young (usually from the age of 0–6 years old), that hasn't been healed yet.

Between the ages of 0–6 years old (otherwise known as 'the imprint years'), you were living in a hypnotic state, otherwise known as a 'theta state' and would have picked up everything around you—from how people behaved to what they were saying. You were like a sponge, soaking everything up, as you were living from your unconscious mind, and it was from there that your buttons started to form.

I know you may have heard people saying or yourself saying "He really pushes my buttons!" You may be wondering what these buttons are. In this context, these buttons are *the doorways to your memories.*

Each button has a feeling, a story and a belief attached to it.

You are probably wondering, 'How come I cannot remember these moments that I felt hurt as a child? And how come my ex is not the real reason I am in pain?' The reason is simple: you created amnesia around the incidents, to overcome and deal with the pain in the moment.

Amnesia and unconscious beliefs

The pain of these moments had to be dealt with in some way or another. The only way you could deal with them in that moment was to fragment the memory, to create amnesia around it, so that you were kept safe. Is there any wonder then that when your ex shows up and pushes on the button that you get angry or upset? Of course not. So the pattern looks something like this:

I often get asked, "Wouldn't life be easier if we could remember what had happened to us as children?" The answer to which is "No". Imagine if you could access all those moments of pain as a child. You wouldn't be able to live! You would live in a constant state of stress and you would not be able to cope.

With every painful moment you experienced as a child, you created a belief around it. These negative beliefs are what attract and recreate situations in your life as your subconscious looks for proof and validation of those beliefs.

Unconscious beliefs are *the meanings you gave to the memories of your past that* you may have perceived as negative. As mentioned in Chapter 3, you are a 'meaning-making' machine.

It is in your nature to want to create some meaning out of everything that happens to you, whether good or bad. But a situation is nothing other than a situation *until you give a positive or negative meaning to it.* It's the *meaning* that will cause you the long-term harm, *not the situation or behaviour itself.*

When you were a child, you may have given meaning to situations, but at such a young age these meanings may easily have been misperceptions. Holding onto these negative, unconscious memories, and the beliefs you made around those moments will, over time, cause a lot more stress in the body and increase the chance of manifesting disease, anxiety, allergies or skin disorders. During my trainings, I have come across a lot of people who have fallen ill with M.E., fibromyalgia and other chronic fatigue-type diseases, influenced by their lopsided perceptions and negative beliefs they have about themselves and their environment.

Bruce Lipton, the father of epigenetics, found that our genes respond to their environment. The environment that you create for your genes will be made up of your unconscious beliefs and (mis)perceptions you had as a child. These misinterpretations will send messages to your cells and if they are negative ones, the cells will receive this information and therefore your body will adapt to its circumstances. So if you are having your buttons pushed by your ex and you are responding negatively based on your unconscious beliefs, you most likely will go into a state of stress as your system feels like you are in danger. Your body then will click into protection/repair mode. We learned in *Chapter 1 Commit* that this means: increased adrenalin, increased cortisol, increased blood sugar levels, increased blood pressure .... all suppressing the immune system. What's the result? Illness and disease.

You also learned that for ultimate health we need to remain in *growth mode.* To do this, you will need to change your perception or negative unconscious beliefs so that you send totally different messages to your cells and reprogram their expression, so you reduce stress. So it's all about starting to change your belief systems.

Imagine your unconscious beliefs and thought patterns are like different computer files. What happens if you upload a corrupted computer file to your computer? Well, for the most part it won't work, and it could corrupt the entire system. Your beliefs are the same. Change the file and the system will start working again.

At one point on my healing journey, I decided to get a check-up and found to my horror that my adrenal stress was sky high. I had been wondering why I had to sleep at least two hours during the day because I was so exhausted. Now, a year on, my adrenals have improved dramatically by taking supplements, working on my perceptions and looking after myself.

Some of the most prevalent unconscious core beliefs I have come across when working with my clients are:

Do any of these seem familiar? If not, you can make up some of your own. The trick is to identify what they are so you can decrease the stress.

Where is the unconscious mind?

Science has found that the unconscious is not stored in the brain but exists in a 'field'. The field is sometimes referred to as 'The Matrix'. In Chapter 2 I briefly mentioned *The Divine Matrix* by Gregg Braden. According to Braden, the Matrix is a field of energy that connects everything and acts as a container and mirror for your beliefs. The field is holographic by nature and each part is connected to all others. Max Planck, the father of quantum physics, discovered that there is a magnetic field between every living thing and that even though you and I cannot see it, *it does actually exist*.

"So what has this got to do with anything?" I hear you cry. Well, anything that you saw, heard or experienced as a child is being held around you, in your energy field. Imagine this invisible field, like the walls of an art gallery, and the images that you have created for yourself as a child are like the paintings on those walls. You have all these images and pictures surrounding your very being, without even knowing it. Each of those paintings will have a name that you gave to each of them that represents the beliefs that you made about yourself, your relationships and the world you live in.

Now, imagine your unconscious as a blank canvas. What would you paint on this blank canvas and, more importantly, what would you call it?

Your blank canvas

EXERCISE: Your Blank Canvas

Take a moment to find a memory that you have from before you were six. Who was there? What was going on? Now, **draw a picture of this memory** then and then **give it a name** that represents the unconscious core belief you have attached to the story. It could perhaps be 'Men I love leave me' or 'The world is a dangerous place'. Just let yourself go here and trust that what you draw and name your picture will be significant to you.

Let me give you an example of one of my core beliefs that I discovered by doing an exercise just like this. I used to believe that if I were not in a relationship with somebody that I would not be worth anything. My self-esteem used to revolve around me being in a relationship with somebody. If I wasn't then that would mean I was worthless. This is why every time a relationship ended, I literally had the feeling that I wanted to die.

Not only did this happen when my ex-husband wanted to end it, but it also happened with my boyfriend when I was in my early twenties. We had been together for four months and he had ended it because I had decided to move to a different university. So distraught was I about the split that I ended up taking more drugs, not eating and drinking on a consistent basis. This continued to the point that just eight weeks into being at my new university, I decided I could not take the pain anymore and that I just wanted to end it all. At that point, I went to the chemist and bought myself some sleeping tablets, went home and swallowed a little over a quarter of them. I lay down and was ready to meet my fate, until I heard a little voice in my head asking *"What have you done?"*

Your ex has come into your life for you to learn something about yourself and, if you are up for it, to heal from the past.

I was then so panicked by what I had done that I dragged myself downstairs and told one of my friends what had happened. She called an ambulance and I was rushed off to hospital to have my stomach pumped. Luckily, I was fine. Although I had to leave university and spend time with my parents, it was the start of my healing journey. Looking back, I can now see the powerful control that an unconscious belief can have on you.

No wonder your buttons get pushed. It's completely normal that you would feel this way. Unresolved pain from the past can feel like you are still living it today. But just remember, as mentioned before, that your ex is *just a trigger and not the source* of the pain you feel.

Your ex has come into your life for you to learn something about yourself and, if you are up for it, to heal from the past. If you don't, you will keep on attracting the same sort of men and relationship situations into your life, and will keep on doing so until you heal.

Beliefs fuel what you attract

Remember I told you that the experiences of your past and the unconscious beliefs you developed at the time will have a direct consequence on what you attract into your life? The Law of Attraction, which works on the basis that the universe responds to consciousness and your thoughts become your reality, means your beliefs will be reflected back to you by your relationships, in this case that with your ex.

The Law of Attraction also works on the basis of energy. Every belief and thought carries its own vibration, its own energy, which, as mentioned, remains in your energy field and thus attracts the same energy. So if you are carrying negative beliefs and thoughts that do not empower you, along with negative images in your head, then *this is what you will attract*, even though *consciously* you don't want to. But, please, do know that even though your unconscious can run the show, *YOU can choose to run it* by changing your beliefs and pictures of the memories of those past experiences. You can create a new painting on your canvas.

Case Study: Lauren

I worked with Lauren, who came to me because she was still struggling to move on from her ex, even though they had split up two years before. She recognized that she had attracted a man who couldn't commit and she was very upset because she wanted to settle down and felt she had lost her opportunity to do so. This upset feeling led her back to a memory where she had found herself similarly upset and scared because her parents had left her at boarding school.

Following the Blank Canvas exercise, the name she gave to this image was 'The People I love, leave'. Was that true? No. We found out that her parents had left her at boarding school because they wanted her to have a good, solid education and, in fact, loved her so much that she was the only one out of her siblings that was given this amazing opportunity. We changed the belief, which had been based on a misconception, to its opposite and now she feels cared for.

As a result of that belief Lauren had repeatedly found it difficult to attract men who would commit. In fact, it had become a reoccurring pattern that had become her *Relationship Pattern Blueprint.*

Your Relationship Pattern Blueprint

What you believe about yourself will be reflected in the sort of relationship you had, or still have, with your ex and the type of men or relationships you have attracted in the past. In order to move forward and not enter into the same sort of relationship again, it is essential that you identify what these beliefs are, as they will determine your relationship success in the future.

Until the wound is healed, you will usually carry on attracting the same sorts of relationships to you, over and over again. These beliefs run your life and in the context of your ex/exes, these beliefs will be driving your Relationship Pattern Blueprint.

A Relationship Pattern Blueprint story: Mine

I had a belief that I was not good enough to have somebody who loved me properly; that somehow I was not worthy of having a good relationship. I would choose to have affairs. This belief was mixed in with the fact there was a history of affairs in the family. As I understand it now, patterns are handed down from generation to generation. We learn from those around us, like our parents, and we unconsciously pick up their behaviours, just as they did from their parents.

My pattern would always start with me falling in love with a kind, blonde man and would then lead to me having an affair with a hot-blooded Latino, and this is what led to the demise of my marriage—as I had a belief that I was not lovable. So whenever a kind man would get close, I would push him away and fall for somebody who didn't care for me, but it was like proof to myself that if I could get a man who was not committed to me to become committed, then I was worthy of love.

My ex-husband and I had been married only for a year. He had proposed on July 4 2005. At the time he was my best friend and someone I looked up to. In November of that year, we got married at New York City Hall and in January 2006, the affair started, by September 2006 we separated and by January 2007 the divorce papers were signed. As you can imagine, it was a very intense time for me.

By the time it came to the wedding, I was between a rock and a hard place. I wanted to cancel but was fearful that my family would find out the real reason why I was cancelling. I did not want him to find out, so I carried on as if nothing was happening. We had also made plans to have a beautiful second ceremony in Spain afterwards, where we had met in the June. So we had an incredible ceremony in Spain, and for that day the nightmare that was going on behind the scenes was all but a distant blur.

Now, I am not proud of what happened. In fact, there was no-one else who judged that woman as harshly as I did. I beat myself day after day for what I had done. I know that I caused a lot of hurt to those around me.

The good news is that I have stopped this pattern. Once I had become aware of it, I finally realized that I would have to change my behaviour and this meant changing the belief around it, which is what I did. I am now in a relationship with an incredible man who treats me very well and who I no longer want to push away because I know that I am lovable.

You see, by not shifting the beliefs, you will most probably keep on with behaviours that appear to prove the unconscious beliefs that you hold. So, how to do this?

How to change your Relationship Pattern Blueprint

As with everything, the first step to change is awareness. Once you have the awareness, you have the power to change what is not working for you. To uncover your Relationship Pattern Blueprint you will need to **discover what your patterns are to uncover the beliefs behind them.** So let's do a little exercise to do just that.

EXERCISE:

Discover your patterns and beliefs.

What I want you to do now is to **sit down and list all your exes** into the table below**.** (Now if you only ever went out with your current ex, list down friendships that you have had challenges with in the past, or are having at this moment.)

Next to each one, **write down the behaviours that would push your buttons.**

Now, write down in the next column **what behavioural pattern you exhibited in response to that behaviour.**

In the column for beliefs, **write down the core belief you have been running as a result.**

Name of my ex	Behaviour that pushed my buttons	How did I act towards him?	What beliefs are showing up?
E.g. Tom	Wouldn't commit	I would walk on egg shells to keep him	Men I love leave

Now **circle the similarities** and then fill in the blanks that I have set out for you below. This is where you **create the awareness**.

- The type of man that I have attracted in my past has been
  ____
  ____
  ____
  ____

- And how I have behaved towards them is
  ____
  ____
  ____
  ____

- What each of them has shown me is
  ____
  ____
  ____
  ____

To find out the memory and to change the belief, you can download your guided visualisation here www.GoodByeMrEx.com/ReliefFromBelief.

So what behaviours and patterns have you come up with? Were there any that surprised you? Don't beat yourself up here—just remember that you were doing the best you could with the resources that you had at the time.

The good news is that by understanding what the beliefs are, you can change them to their opposite. Now, do you start to see how your ex can be the start to your healing journey? Do you see that he is not the source of your anger, jealousy, guilt, frustration or of any other perceived negative emotions you may have? He is just the trigger—a gift that (as annoying as he might be) has given you the opportunity to learn, to see your patterns, and grow and heal from your past.

As long as you are willing to do the work—you will get there.

INQUIRE to challenge assumptions and expectations

"Don't Make Assumptions. Find the courage to ask questions and to express what you really want. With just this one agreement, you can completely transform your life."

Miguel Angel Ruiz

"Disappointment is a sort of bankruptcy—the bankruptcy of a soul that expends too much in hope and expectation."

William Shakespeare

As you can see from these quotes, both assumptions and expectations are termites to any relationship. They will also drive you absolutely balmy! As the first quote says, challenge your **assumptions** with questions! The second quote illustrates that **expectations** also need to be challenged if you want to remove yourself from the constant feelings of disappointment you may experience.

This chapter is all about solving these key factors that would keep you stuck in your disappointment and frustration—it is about *challenging your assumptions and expectations.*

Assumptions

So let's start with assumptions. In my view, assumptions are about second-guessing what your ex is doing or thinking, or even what his ulterior motives are.

When I am coaching my private clients I often need to challenge their notion that they knew what their ex was thinking and whether or not his action had any malicious intent behind it. Maybe it did and *maybe it didn't.*

The answer I give them every time is "*You just don't know*". And that is the truth.

You may never know why he left or why he behaves or behaved the way he did; unless you actually get underneath his skin, you will never ever know.

The only way we could truly understand another human being (other than asking them) would be to actually become them—to be born as them, to grow up as them, to have exactly the same experiences, thoughts, environment and influences as them.

An incredible example that makes this stand out for me is the story that a client told me about her family. For many years she had grown to hate her father because she believed that he was having an affair. She would hear him sneaking out in the middle of the night and come back in the early morning for quite a few years. She expressed this to her brother who had also become to despise their father. The children now would take sides and would always defend their mother because they felt it was unfair that she had to live with such disloyalty.

Finally, she and her brother decided to confront their mother about it before saying anything to their father, out of fear. Their mother took in the information and decided that it was time to have the truth come out. They called a family meeting and were finally confronted with the truth.

As it turns out their father had been leaving home every night to work as a janitor. He had been struggling to find a new job and was too ashamed to say anything to his children. His wife knew, but he couldn't face disappointing his children. He had been working hard to ensure that he could provide. His wife had known but, like him, didn't want to say anything because they didn't want to worry the children.

As you can imagine the children were somewhat confused and in shock about his motives, but were finally able to see the truth.

As this story illustrates, assumptions are just fantasies and, before you know it, you are consumed by the upset and the lies that you have told yourself.

You may have made the assumption that your ex will respond in the same way to things as you would, or that he has the same way of dealing with the separation as you. Does he really? Or is this just an assumption? This can lead to more arguments and misunderstandings, which can make matters worse for you.

This is completely normal by the way. Assumptions are what we do best as human beings. Your mind will want to justify, rationalize and search for the answers to understand everything, just to feel safe. The reasoning mind automatically wants to have all its ducks in a row, to make sure it knows what is going on at any particular time. These assumptions are made hard and fast, and most of the time unconsciously.

So what are some classic examples of assumptions that you may have made? The ones that I find to be most common among my clients are:

- If he had really cared about the relationship with me, he wouldn't have....
- If he really cared about his children, he wouldn't...
- If he ever cared or loved me, he would know what I want and how I feel.

How could he have done ... after all I did for him?

Getting personal with assumptions

The other problem with making an assumption is that it is the fuel to making things personal, especially if the assumption has a negative connotation to it, which in most cases it will.

Let me give you an example. Say to yourself "If he really cared about the relationship, he wouldn't have_______" (fill in the blank). In just saying that to yourself, how does it make you feel? Probably not so great, right? With these sorts of assumptions, it now becomes 'about you'; you take them on as if they are the truth, and make it personal.

But it's not about you!

I know this is probably a hard pill to swallow, but it's about him and his world. It's about his inner beliefs and how his world and his mind work. When you take something personally you are making the assumption he knows what is going on with you, which he doesn't! What he does or doesn't do, and what he says or doesn't say, will be based on his education, gender, experience, beliefs, values and opinions, and how he views and perceives the world. When you assume, you are *projecting your world onto his* and he will do the same. No one's is better or worse; they are just different.

I am sure that you are wondering *But, Marina, how can I not take personally the fact that he ignores me or that he doesn't look after the kids properly?* Well, that is his stuff, not yours. You can take it on if you want, but this is what will cause your suffering and pain.

You will feel rejected and upset and feel that your self-worth is tied to him—but it's not! Rejection is never personal. Your self-worth is tied to you, and how you feel about you will be linked to the beliefs and self-image you have. The difference between somebody who can get over someone more quickly than somebody else is usually directly linked to what and how they see themselves.

CASE STUDY: My Ex—Paul

In March 2011, Paul (the second relationship I was in after my divorce) split up with me and left me to pick up the pieces, I took it all really personally. How could I not, right? His leaving was devastating. The fact that he suddenly left one day without warning, led me to assume he didn't care—that somehow, I had done something wrong or didn't warrant a better explanation from him. However, a few months down the line, I realized that the way he chose to leave was based upon the resources he had at his disposal at the time. *He couldn't have done it any other way, otherwise he would have.*

I am not excusing his behaviour, but I later found out that he left the way he did, because he thought it would be less of a blow for me. Rather than dragging it out and having me watch him leave, he felt it would it made things clear cut. As you know now, if he had done it any other way there would have been just as many drawbacks as benefits to me anyway.

Occasionally, we would text, and what was really interesting to me was that those texts made no sense to me. It was like I was talking to an alien. And that is when it sunk in. *He is not me, I think differently, he feels differently and he sees his life through completely different eyes to me.* You might find it is the same for your ex.

So let's do an exercise to help you stop taking rejection so personally.

•

Rejection is never personal

Exercise:

1) **Now create a mantra for yourself to say that 'rejection is never personal'.** Stick it on a piece of paper on your fridge, on your phone, anywhere you will see it on a daily basis **and say it to yourself over and over until you start to believe it.**

Just as assumptions will keep you stuck, this can create and ingrain a new line of belief. Do this over a period of 21 days and you will reap the benefits, just as my client Lauren did.

By doing this exercise she kept track of when she was making assumptions on, and it stopped her from doing so.

Expect the unexpected from expectations

"*Expectation is the root of all heartache.*" ~ William Shakespeare

The definition of an expectation according to the Oxford Dictionary is ***'a strong belief that something will happen or be the case in the future.'*** When you have an expectation, you are actually living a fantasy—creating a future for yourself that hasn't happened yet.

With these sorts of thoughts, the chances are that you will feel disappointed and frustrated when how it does play out (if it does) is less than how you built it up in your mind. The chances are that the situation will never be as good. How can it be? Fantasies are never as great on paper as they are in your head.

Did you feel disappointed by your ex's behaviour? Did you feel disappointed by the fact that you no longer would have the future you thought you would have with him? The one major disappointment and hurt my clients feel is that they will no longer have the life they expected to have with him. Because what they expected to happen hasn't, and cannot, all of their dreams are shattered. However, they have no idea of what sort of life they would have had with him, if they had carried on in the relationship.

Now, *if he creates expectations for you* by saying he will do things and doesn't, then it makes sense that you will be disappointed and frustrated when he doesn't follow through. Unfortunately, you cannot control him, *you can only control you.* You may be thinking to yourself, *But, Marina what about the disappointment he has created around the kids?* Well, as you know by now—there is never a negative without a positive. *Look for the gift* in him not doing what he said he was going to do.

So, what can you do to ensure that you don't keep yourself feeling frustrated and disappointed? The best way is to inquire.

CASE STUDY: Joan

One of my clients, Joan, tended to go back to her 'expecting' pattern a lot during our sessions. Her ex left her for another woman and during the divorce process he was somewhat shut-off from Joan. Her expectations of how they were going to live their future was upsetting her. She had not realised that she was taking his behaviour on and making it personal to her.

We had a long discussion about this and she got to finally see that he was his own person, with his own strategies and belief systems, just as her behaviour was the result of her beliefs, gender, education and values—and she may have pressed his buttons

We discussed how he was like a different land from her, just like people in Spain, where they have dinner late and tend to want to tell you how to do things, are different to, let's say we Brits in the UK, who are more reserved and have dinner earlier because of the weather and our upbringing. The same was true of her ex; he was doing what he could with the resources he had.

However, this discussion didn't change her feelings overnight. She had to practice and be aware that every time she was going into her expectation pattern, to realise that she was doing just that, so that she didn't get sucked into the drama that was going on for her in her head. She then asked some very powerful questions that got her to realise that she was just projecting her own thoughts onto him.

This really helped her challenge the expectations that she kept on creating, but it was by practicing that she was able to form it into a habit. The more you ask these questions, the more they will come to you automatically; *they will become part of who you are.* Does that make sense?

It's like riding a bicycle. At first you had conscious incompetence—where you were falling around all the time. Then you started to become more competent but there were certain parts to riding the bike that you still needed to be conscious of, otherwise you would fall. Then through practising, you found yourself one day not even thinking about it anymore. It had become part of who you were. That is *unconscious competence.* When you no longer have to think about what you are doing. It just comes naturally.

So what were these powerful questions?

Inquiry by asking powerful questions

"An unquestioned mind is the world of suffering." **~ Byron Katie**

A powerful question will challenge your usual way of thinking. It is like taking a short cut. You will have your own thought patterns and your own ways of thinking that take you down the same road every day, to the same destination.

What if you could take a different route home that got you there faster? Powerful questions are your short cut to challenging your assumptions and expectations. One powerful question can change your life.

I have had many moments like this in my life. But some of the most powerful questions that I have experienced are as a result of author Byron Katie's work in *Loving What Is*. Her work is simple and yet powerful. She challenges the innermost thoughts we have.

When I went to her seminar in London, it really got me to be aware of the thoughts that I think and what I need to do to challenge the assumptions I create for myself. On stage she was facilitating this one lady who believed that her father was cold towards her, as he had not come to the hospital to see her. What she realized by asking these questions was that it wasn't actually true. She realized that he did, but it was her coldness that was stopping him from coming close as he felt rejected by her.

So why don't you have a go?

EXERCISE: How can I know it's true?

Write down an expectation or assumption that you have created around your ex.

Then challenge it by asking the following questions:

Q1: "Is it really true?"

Q2: "Can I absolutely know its true?"

Q3: "What happens when I believe that thought?"

Q4: "Who would I be without that thought?"

Turn the assumption or expectation around – Use "I" instead of he or him and find 3 examples of where you do xyz for each of the new statements.

By asking yourself these questions you can challenge your expectation and lessen the disappointment.

By doing this you will be able to challenge your thinking patterns and lessen your own suffering.

FOCUS ON LANGUAGE AND COMMUNICATION

"In between stimulus and response there is a space.
In that space lies our power to choose our response.
In our response lies our growth and our freedom."

Victor Frankl

Until now I have given you lots of tools that can help you when your ex is not around. When he has done something, or said something, that has hurt or upset you, you are now able to use the exercises that I have given you to calm yourself down and to balance your state. The purpose of this chapter is for you to shift your focus onto your *language* and *communication* so you can turn your conflictive reality into one of softness.

This chapter tackles the conundrum of communication both within yourself and with your ex. If you currently have contact with your ex, these communication techniques will really help you. If you don't have contact with him anymore, you can always use the techniques in your next relationship.

If you find yourself angry and resentful, or upset at yet another argument, *be honest with yourself and ask yourself which of your own behaviours could be exacerbating the situation?* Could it be that you are making demands? Are you shouting? Blaming? These behaviours externalize the problem, so you are avoiding taking responsibility and are focusing on what your ex is doing or not doing.

Blaming and shaming

GOOD BOOKS CAN HELP

By blaming and shaming, your heart closes off and you stay in judgement and criticism, which can magnify your fear, allowing your monkey brain to go crazy and stop you from thinking clearly.

Blame also blocks communication. Did you blame your ex when you split? Are you still blaming and shaming him now? Is he doing it to you? Have you seen how doing this can close each of you down, while it adds more stress to the pot?

Blame is known to be one of the four grim reapers of relationship communication. The others are *contempt, criticism* and *stonewalling* (shutting down emotionally).

It makes sense. What do you do when you feel under attack? Some of us will retaliate and fight back. Some of us will take flight and hide. Our reaction to the reactive behaviour of blame will introduce us to the reptilian brain (the oldest part of the brain) that protects our own survival. Reactive behaviours are about survival. When emotions are high, intelligence is low and this is why we react.

Where do these reactions come from?

These reactions will come from, and be pre-set to, *when you were six years old or less.* I used to deal with stressful situations by hiding in the bathroom and crying, and this is what I used to do as a child too. There was no harm in it, but just observe that this is where these behaviours come from.

You may have noticed by now that the only thing you have control over is *yourself.* Wishing and wanting your ex to act in a different way and to change makes matters worse for your frustrations and for the whole dynamic.

After all, frustrations are another way of saying "I want him to be different and act in a different way, but he won't." You get tied into these thoughts, and as he does not change and continues doing what he has always done, you get angrier and judge him.

I know for a fact that this does not work!

I understand that the reactions you have been expressing for years are very powerful, as you have been practising them diligently for years, over and over again, and now they have become a habit. However...

"If you do what you've always done, you'll get what you've always gotten." ~ Anthony Robbins.

I love this quote as it sums up what will happen if you keep on doing what you are doing, even when it is not working for you.

Fight or flight response

When you experience excessive stress—whether from internal worry or external circumstance—a bodily reaction is triggered called the 'fight or flight response'. Originally discovered by the great Harvard physiologist Walter Cannon, this response is hardwired into your brain and represents a genetic wisdom designed to protect you from bodily harm. This response actually corresponds to an area of your brain called the 'hypothalamus', which—when stimulated—initiates a sequence of nerve cell firing and chemical release that prepares your body for running or fighting.

Your fight or flight response is designed to protect the stone-age you from the proverbial sabre-toothed tigers that once lurked in the woods and fields around you, threatening your physical survival. At times when your actual physical survival is threatened, there is no greater response to have on your side.

If you change your behaviour, your ex will change his.

In some instances in these modern times, these primordial responses are effective, but if they are not helping with your dynamic, it's time to choose a different behaviour. And the truth is your behaviour will influence your ex's behaviour.

You may think *But I do nothing and he still acts up.* But even if this is the case, it would be a good idea to find out what it is you were doing or not doing that might have triggered him.

Just like you, your ex will have his own triggers. He will also have things he will want to blame you for and parts of himself he has disowned that he may not be willing to look at, which gets him angry and has him judging you.

Nothing ever happens in a vacuum. You are part of a dynamic. If you change your reaction, he will change his.

The Law of Cause and Effect

Let me explain what the Law of Cause and Effect is talking about. Whatever you put out you will receive back, and whatever your ex is putting out there will also be given back to him.

You may be thinking right now *But Marina, I don't do anything and he still manages to get wound up and angry or upset, so how does that work?* Well, sometimes doing nothing can trigger him. The key here is to be aware of what you are doing when, and if, you spiral into a conflictive situation.

Let me give you an example. If a woman is sitting at a bar and a man suddenly comes onto her, she may not be altogether innocent. He may have been triggered by the way that she was looking at him or the sexual energy that she was putting out to him. He may have thought to himself *This woman is looking at me in a sexual way, and I kinda like her so I will come onto her*—and bam—there he goes. Now she may think *Geesh, I did nothing to bring this on; what a nutter!* But in effect something she did had triggered the reaction. If she reacts quickly and blames him for coming onto him rather than asking herself the question "What part did I play?" she won't know how to correct herself next time. And more than likely she will continue to attract men that she doesn't want to come onto her

The question to ask yourself is: *What can I do to respond rather than react*?

To do so restores your choice to act creatively and serves to decrease your outer and inner conflict and stress, and brings you more peace of mind. An important ingredient in choosing to respond is the language you choose to communicate.

Negative communication patterns and language

Scientific research shows that language and social centres of the brain are not fully mature until you are thirty years old! This means that until you are thirty years old, your ability to be aware of the language you use and how it affects others is fairly limited.

Your language creates your reality.

There are, however, ways in which you can train yourself so you can enhance your communication with others and reduce your conflict and stress. **There are certain communication styles that can stimulate empathy and trust in your listener and interrupt negative thought patterns in the brain.** If you leave these *negative thought patterns* unchecked, they can damage your emotional regulation circuits, which can further your stress levels and feelings of powerlessness. So, lets look at the language of some of the most popular communication patterns that will bring about a negative result.

He 'never' ... he 'always'

Using exaggerations such as 'never' or 'always' will cancel out the times when he does do that very thing that you 'never' or 'always' perceive him to do. You see, *what you focus on expands!* That's right. If you are focusing on the fact that your ex NEVER does something, he won't. If you focus on the fact that he ALWAYS does something, guess what? He will.

Yes, your language will create your reality and by using this language of 'he never' and 'he always' you will be creating a black and white existence instead of one of a shade of grey where your ex is not the *all or nothing* person that you perceive him to be. Using that exaggerated language is like being on a pendulum—going from NEVER to ALWAYS—that doesn't reach the middle point.

The 'you are' and 'he is' syndrome

Another negative communication pattern I see most of my clients use, and I have done so myself, is to *make his behaviour all of who he is*. We define our ex by his behaviour, by using the 'you are' or 'he is' clause. You may find yourself saying things about him to your friends like "He is so pathetic"; "He is so lazy"; "He is so selfish"; or "He is such a liar".

The challenge you have with using this language is that your ex's behaviour now becomes all of who he is, rather than just relating to his behaviour. You learnt in Chapter Two that he is not one-sided, but rather is a balance of two sides: selfish/generous, lazy/motivated, a liar/an honest person.

Defining his behaviour as being the issue (as opposed to all of him), will help you remember that he is not one-sided and will give you a more realistic perspective. You won't be dragged down by your own misperceptions. For example, rather than saying "He is selfish" you could say "He did a selfish act".

Now, when you read these two statements—"He is selfish" and "He did a selfish thing"—how does the first *make you feel* compared to the second? Be honest with yourself here. Does the first make you feel angrier than the second?

Here we are focussing on shifting your focus away from wide, sweeping generalizations that only serve to aggravate you even more.

He makes me feel...

Another one to watch out for is the 'He makes me feel' clause.

***"No one can create negativity or stress within you. Only you can do that by virtue of how you process your world."* ~ Wayne Dyer**.

I often hear my clients say that *he makes them feel this way or that way*—but by virtue of who they are and the experiences they have had in the past, you can see now that you choose what meaning to give to his actions and then you create the negative emotion in yourself,

Thoughts • Feelings • Behaviour

Overall, my point here is if you change your thoughts around the behaviour of your ex, then the chances are you will reduce the feeling. It's very likely that you have an ingrained negative belief behind how you perceive what he has done or not done and you can change this by being mindful of how you communicate about him and with him.

So far we've focussed on negative ways in which you think and communicate about your ex. Now let's look at how to communicate more effectively with him directly by applying some balanced patterns of communication—Remember, the goal of all this is so that you can move on!

How to communicate positively with your ex

When you get angry or upset at him for something he has done, there are a couple of techniques that will help you to create a safe space where you can express what you need to, in a way that will more likely open him up to listen.

Express how you feel and what you need. By expressing *how you feel* about his behaviour, it gives you time to explore your own internal world, so you can uncover why you feel the way you do and express your frustration and hurt in a way that empowers you. By asking for *what you need*, you will find out why you feel the way you do and what it is you are searching for. You will more than likely get a more favourable response from your ex as he won't get his back up.

Make requests versus make demands. Making a demand can sound like blame and punishment to the listener. By making a request, you are removing the demand from the equation. As you have probably already found out, you cannot *make anybody do anything*, least of all the person who is supposed to be 'the enemy'. Laying demands on your ex, such as "I want you to pick up the children" or "I want you to pay the money into my account by..." will bring out more resentment on his side, just as it would for you if you were on the receiving end.

Making a request does not involve reprimanding the other person if they decide not to go ahead with the idea. The trick is to have NO attachment to the outcome. If you do, they will hear your requests as demands and instinctively want to protect themselves.

Let's put these two techniques into practice...

EXERCISE:
Positive Communication Practice

What I would like you to do right now is to **write down a scenario** where you felt let down by your ex and you got angry, and write down what you did. Then I want you to go through these following steps:

Write down how you felt about his behaviour. For example: "I felt angry", or "I felt hurt", or "I felt overwhelmed".

Write down what you need from him. For example: "I felt really disappointed when you didn't pick up the children because I need to have the peace of mind that things are sorted when we arrange them."

In this example, by focusing attention on your own feelings and needs, you become conscious that your current feeling of hurt derives from your need for peace of mind,

Write down what you need from him next time and indicate that you only want him to comply if he is willing to do so. For example, "Would you be willing to pick up the kids from school?" vs. "I would like you to pick up the kids from school".

If he answers no, **show empathy towards his decision** and ask why he can't. This will show that you are really making a request.

Do this for different scenarios that are repeated time and time again. Once you have them written down, practise them over and over, so they become automatic.

I know it may feel a little forced at the beginning; however, it's like riding a bicycle. It just needs practice. Some people might even think it to be manipulative, but it will only feel like this because you are not used to doing it. Although there is a common belief that good communication comes naturally, it isn't the case. Good and effective communication skills need to be nurtured and worked on.

Case Study: A quick story

I worked with a client who used these techniques and the results for her were incredible. She came to me as she was frustrated that her ex wouldn't communicate with her about their break-up. She desperately wanted answers and wasn't getting the outcome she wanted.

I took her through all the steps and when it came to this situation, we explored how she was communicating with him. It was obvious she was coming from a position of blaming him for what had happened and was communicating that to him, plus demanding answers from him. As a man, he just scuttled away into his cave and didn't want to come out.

Once we worked with this, she could see how her behaviour was not serving her and him and that even though she was no longer blaming herself, she still wanted to express herself in a way so that they could communicate without the argument or without him ignoring her. At this point we decided to write him a letter (with the same format as the exercise above). A few weeks later, he responded and provided her with all the information and insights she was after, but from a totally different viewpoint than what she could have imagined. In his experience, things were seen in a different way completely.

Listen and cocoon yourself

The powerful communication tool that I am talking about is *listening*. By listening, you automatically become present and your need to defend dissolves. If you find yourself in another confrontation, go in with the intention that you will just listen to what he has to say. In your mind's eye, visualize a bubble around you so that you won't take on his 'stuff'. Breathing in his anger and resentment will hurt you and leave you feeling worse.

What I have done in the past, and have asked clients to do too, is to imagine that they are in a protective bright white light cocoon, so no matter what anger is being thrown at them, the anger and hurt can just bounce off them. I have created an audio for you to download so that at any time you want to protect yourself you can. To access my free White Light Cocoon download go to www.GoodByeMrEx.com/WhiteLightCocoon.

A white light cocoon story

I had an incredible experience of this when I had to have a difficult conversation With my ex, George – the same George who taught me to stand on my own two feet and who I found challenging to let go. We had not spoken for six months, as he was angry at the fact that I had ended our relationship and had rushed into a new one with Paul (the second serious relationship I had after my divorce).

I finally plucked up the courage to speak to him and resolve the unresolved, as I wanted to clear the air. However, I finally called him and you could have cut the air with a knife. It then went from tension to civil; from civil to warm. By the end we decided to meet.

Until this point we had not spoken about what had happened and I thought that he had resolved it; but I was wrong. Suddenly he asked me about my love life, which then opened up the doorway to his anger and hurt. As he expressed his anger at me, I instinctively wanted to defend myself but I heard the inner voice, which said "SHUT UP AND LISTEN TO HIM!"

So, instead I imagined a shield of white light protecting me while I listened. As I sat and *really* listened to what he had to say, my desire to be right subsided and in its place welled up feelings of empathy where I started to feel his pain and anger. As I listened more intently, he felt heard and validated. Towards the end of his expressing what he needed to, I repeated his statements back to him to ensure that I had understood what he had said, I then validated his position by saying, "That must have been hard for you. I completely get why you feel angry and lied to."

By the end, his physiology changed and his anger and frustration transformed into calmness, and reconciliation followed suit.

Most of the time, we do not get to fully express ourselves in a safe environment where each and every voice is heard and validated; but when it happens, it's magic.

If you are in a position of not wanting to talk to each other at all and it is too difficult, then maybe see if you can get in a third party to help you both out. The key here is to understand *who and what you are doing this for*. If it is going to help your kids or you still have to see each other because you have a business together, do it for the kids or for the business. If you are not in contact with him anymore, you can always use these techniques in your next relationship too.

TRANSFORM THROUGH GRATITUDE

"Gratitude is another way of saying 'a GREAT ATTITUDE'. To do that, you have to EAT the ATTITUDE."

Marina Pearson

This next chapter will help you let go of the 'if only's' and 'what if's' that keep you regretting the past and fearing your future. Being in this state will guarantee you staying stuck. By using the art of gratitude and the processes I lay out here, you will find that the regret and fear will dissolve, leaving you feeling grateful for how things are.

Now, I know that you are probably wondering, *Marina, how can I be grateful for what has happened? Especially after everything that he has done to make my life a complete misery? And now, I am left with the fear of being alone and the guilt of wishing I had something more.*

I think this following quote sums it up for me:

"Whether you pushed me or pulled me, drained me or fuelled me, loved me or left me, hurt me or helped me, you are a part of my growth, and no kidding, I thank you!" **- Anon**

I get that this is something to be somewhat perplexed about, but you can get there. By now, if you have been doing the exercises, you will have started to feel differently about your ex. The final piece of the puzzle is only just a step away and will have you feeling completely at peace for what is and not wanting to change your ex nor his behaviour.

Gratitude—the key to transformation

Gratitude is such a profound word. For me personally, gratitude has helped me free myself from living in a place of lack, to really focusing on what I have. The daily practice of gratitude is the secret to freeing you from the shackles of the past and really moving you into the present.

Lao Tzu Tung said it all:

"If you are depressed, you are living in the past. If you are anxious, you are living in the future. If you are at peace, you are living in the present." **~ Lao Tzu**

Gratitude will enable you to truly appreciate what you have, not what you don't. I was always looking at the gaps. Living in London, I am always reminded of this as I hear the guy on the Tube saying "Mind the Gap". You can easily fall into the gaps of discontent and focus on what your ex is *not* doing, or has not done, instead of what he has. That is what I *used to* do.

Gratitude goes beyond acceptance and beyond politeness. It is a feeling of complete grace. It is a moment when your heart is open and there is no judgement, nor resentment; where you are at peace with what is. It is when your perceptions have come into complete balance and you are able to see both the upsides and the downsides of him and the situation you find yourself in.

Your biggest challenges are what make you grow and learn—and if you are not growing, you are dying. To think that you will NEVER have challenges and that life will be plain sailing is a fantasy. You will ALWAYS have both. Support and challenge will come in equal measure, as this is what love is about.

How to attract more of what you want!

But your mind will tend to focus on what you don't have. As I have already mentioned, what you focus on expands, so train your mind to focus on those things that you do have. I have found that the more I do that, the more I receive that wonderful stuff. Every state you find yourself experiencing, whether it be sadness, anger, gratitude or peace, will be giving out an energy—and energy has a vibration, right?

Gratitude is one of those states with a high vibration that will attract more people and things to you that you can be more grateful for!

The trick here is that things like sadness, anger and resentment are states that vibrate at low frequency, and you will attract things and people to you that vibrate at a similar frequency. You are, however, an unlimited being full of potential, and you can raise your vibration to attract some cool stuff to you, if you know how.

Gratitude is one of those states with a high vibration that will attract more people and things to you that you can be more grateful for!

Shifting your perceptions around your ex is the key to start seeing the things you have, instead of focusing on what isn't there. After all, everything is perfect, even if your conscious brain tells you it is not. As I mentioned right at the beginning of the book, unless you are grateful for your ex, you will be dealing with the repercussions of it, either in the form of stress, not being able to attract the relationship you want, or even in the difficulty of being present in the relationship that you may be in (if you are). Or, maybe there are other issues that you are living through as a result.

If you can close your eyes and just say to him (or all your exes) "Thank you for being perfect as you were; I wouldn't have had it any other way" then you know that you are in a place of gratitude. If you are still not able to do this then you know you are not.

Dissolve fear of the future to find your soul mate

"***Your senses are not fully wise. They say what they experience but not the reason why."*** ~ **Aristotle**

When I have had clients come to me, struggling to move on from the pain of their ex, the thing they are often experiencing is the fear of either not finding somebody again or of not being able to have children; or they miss their ex or their children when they are not with them.

Which category do you fall within?

What if the things that you thought were missing are actually already all around you, but in a form that you are not easily able to recognize? Your senses are not able to see things as they are and this is why recognizing the form they are in is a challenge. I certainly struggled with this; however, understanding the first law of thermodynamics is key to this concept.

The first law of thermodynamics states:

"Energy can be changed from one form to another, but it cannot be created or destroyed. The total amount of energy and matter in the Universe remains constant, merely changing from one form to another. Energy is always conserved; it cannot be created or destroyed. In essence, energy can be converted from one form into another."

As you are made up of energy and human beings are made up of energy, people and the aspects you miss about them are in fact in your life 24/7, meaning that somebody else in your life now expresses these traits.

Ralph Waldo Emerson puts it so succinctly:

***"For everything that you have missed, you have gained something else, and for everything you gain, you lose something else."* ~ Ralph Waldo Emerson**

For example, if you fear not being with somebody again, what could be one of the characteristics you would like a new man to have? Is it that you want support? If so, look to see where the support is NOW in your life. Who expresses that for you? Is it your family? Is it your work? Colleagues?

Now, if you see you have support, for example, from your family, it is not enough to just feel grateful for what you have because your mind will still not see what the upsides are of having the support in your family or what the downsides would be of having it in a new relationship. Currently your mind will be saying "Hey, there are more downsides to me having the support in my family and work, than in having it in any future relationship." But this is NOT true.

How do I know it's not true? Because I have experienced it first hand and I have seen my clients go through the process too. There will be just as many upsides to having support in your family as there will be downsides to having it in the new man.

Just like water, if you boil it, it changes form. Characteristics of people are the same.

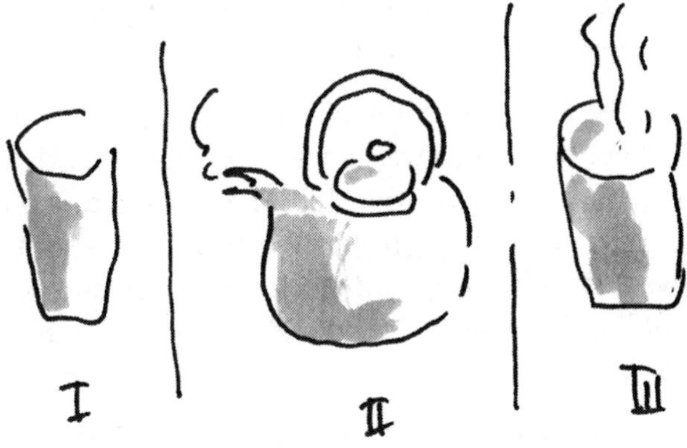

Let me give you an example with the story of Cheryl.

CASE STUDY:
How Cheryl found her soulmate

Cheryl was very fearful of being alone as she believed that she wouldn't find another person. She had images of growing old on her own. By challenging this notion, and by writing down all the things that she wanted in the new relationship such as connection, support and companionship, she realized that she *already* had all of these factors in her life.

She started to see that the *connection* she so much yearned for was actually already being expressed with her cat, her friends, her books and herself. The *support* she was looking for was expressed by her family, friends, me, her business coach, colleagues at work and her cat, and the *companionship* she was yearning for was expressed in her and her friends.

She then looked at how having the support from her friends and family was more beneficial to her than having it in a future relationship. She realized that the support she was getting from all of these people in her life was actually bringing her closer to her purpose of building a business that would help lots of people overcome stress.

She also realized that this was helping her open up spiritually, and allowing her to grow into an empowered business leader. In turn, it was furthering her growth and intuitive insight, which would help all the people that she in turn, works with.

The support within herself has also made her self-sufficient and given her the belief that she can accomplish anything she wants to. She can come and go as she pleases and can pick and choose who she spends her time with.

Furthermore, she also discovered that having all that support in just one person would be suffocating for her and that she would run the risk of being held back by him, as well as not growing in the same way as she is growing at the moment. She could see too that she would probably become dependent on his support and might take advice from him (as somebody that was not an expert in their field), adding financial consequences into the mix.

As we went through the process, the fear turned into relief and by the end, her relief turned into gratitude—a transformation occurred, just like the example of the water boiling and becoming steam. She was overcome with gratitude as she started to realize that everything she wanted to experience in the future was already here and exactly in the way she wanted to experience it. By dissolving the fear, she was no longer a slave to it.

Everything is perfect: My own experience

When Paul left me, I was angry, resentful and above all, really hurt. Even though I knew consciously that somehow I had attracted this loss into my life, I couldn't see how it was actually serving me.

I didn't want to see what was just around the corner, as we had made so many plans. Selfishly, I did not want to admit that my dreams of having a family with him would be crushed. One night we were chatting away on Skype, as I was away, and he told me things had to change, I knew in that moment that he was saying that he wanted to end it. So I asked him whether I was reading the situation right, to which he responded, "Yes." It came as a shock. But now, looking back, the signs had been there but I just did not want to see them.

He moved out two days later. That threw me into a state of even more shock as he had promised to stay until I got back. But what I found interesting at the time was that on the night he moved out, George and I were having our conversation and we made peace.

This event took me right back to how I felt when I was looking at the floor of the Beth Israel Hospital in New York City when I nearly took my life. I started smoking again, even though I hadn't smoked since my divorce, five years previously. Once again I was triggered. For six weeks I couldn't focus. I stopped working, I stopped eating and I felt anxious all the time.

It shook every foundation I had. The image I kept getting was that I was standing in the middle of a war zone where all the houses and buildings around me had been burnt down. My father had also died two months before and I think at that moment everything caught up with me. But even my dad's death had not caused this amount of pain in me.

Once again, I found myself having another dark night of the soul experience. I couldn't believe it was happening again. The difference this time, however, was that I now had the tools to work it through and the conscious awareness to deal with what was happening.

So I used the process that I will show you shortly. I wrote down all the things I missed about him. I then made a list of who was in my life at the time, expressing those things that I missed about him. I then balanced out my perception, to finally experience gratitude for him leaving, as I could see how I had everything in the way I wanted it.

Let me explain further.

After he left, I started to blossom and look after myself in a way I had never done before. First, I went to see a stylist who helped me choose clothes that made me feel like a million bucks. I then decided to learn from what had happened.

I studied male and female dynamics and realized that for most of my life, when in relationships, I had been going into my masculine aspect. This in turn would hinder our intimacy and have the man beside me feel inadequate, as he felt that he couldn't protect me.

One of the things I missed most about Paul was the way he took care of how he dressed (generally, a more feminine aspect) and what I realized was that when he left, I took it on! I also realized how it had benefitted me to take on that feminine part in a new form. I actually had finally stepped into my woman power, by dressing up more, and embraced that part of me that had long been forgotten—and it felt great.

I also realized that I had stopped travelling internationally as much as I would have liked. Our travels would take us to see his kids but would limit where we could go internationally. Once he left, I started to travel again and haven't stopped since!

One of the other things I really missed about him was his family. So I asked myself where in my present environment is that family, the energy of support that I missed. Where did it come back in and how did this serve me? I saw that it was now coming in the form of my friends who supported me through this time.

I also missed Paul caring for me, but I realized that I was now doing it myself by finally deciding to look after my health and to get tests done to find out why I was tired all the time and my hair was thinning so much.

After doing this process, I got to see how perfect everything actually was. I continued to take better care of myself and I stopped missing him. I also realized that I had been infatuated with him, seeing more of his upsides than his downsides; but once I was able to see both, I came into deep gratitude for how it truly was.

The following exercise from Dr John Demartini, a human behavioural specialist and founder of the Demartini Institute and the creator of *The Breakthrough*, has helped me and my clients immensely.

EXERCISE:

'Everything is Perfect' Exercise

Step 1: Write down the aspects you miss about your ex or your kids, or the aspects you would like in a new relationship e.g. support, connection, sense of humour

Step 2: Write down who or what expresses this aspect now (at least 5 people, or until you are certain that the trait was replaced) e.g. is it you, your family, or maybe a stranger on the street?

Step 3: Write down how having each aspect in the new way serves you and serves the top 3 important factors in your life (at least 5 reasons).

Once you can see how the new aspect *really does honour what you want*, move on to step 4.

Step 4: Write down why having each aspect in the old way hinders you and hinders the top 3 important factors in your life (at least 5 reasons).

You will know when you are done when you no longer yearn for your situation to be any different. You will see how the new form serves you and how the old form doesn't.

You will also see how what you perceive to be missing in you may just have gone elsewhere for the time being—the energy is presenting itself through somebody or something else. But by doing this little exercise, you will get to see *where it has gone and why*.

CASE STUDY:

Suzy and her story after she used the Everything is Perfect exercise

Suzy was a nurse who was looking after my mother in her home. She came to me as she felt extremely guilty that she was not with her children in Poland. She was working in the UK and felt that they were worse off as a result of her decision to go there for work. By the end of our process together, however, she could see that everything was actually perfect the way it was. Her children were, in fact, in a much more privileged position and she was doing something she loved and was expressing her love by sending them money to put them through their education.

What you perceive to be missing in you may just have gone elsewhere for the time being—the energy is presenting itself through somebody or something else.

She realized that being with her kids in Poland would have meant she wouldn't have learnt English, nor sought her own independence, and that she would have probably felt frustrated and taken it out on her kids. She discovered that her children had never missed out on having carers OR loving family attention. They were well cared for by their grandparents, aunt and uncle, and not only did they have this family support, but they also were getting a good education, which in Poland is a privilege.

She also felt guilty thinking that her son didn't have a father figure. Of course, this was not true, as you also know by now, nothing is missing—it was just in a form she did not recognize. That form was his uncle. For a while she had perceived that her son was worse off for having his uncle around rather than his father. But as I challenged her on her thinking, she suddenly saw how amazing it was that her brother had taught her son to ski, and he had spent a lot of quality time with him. He had been there for him all along!

When she was truly honest with herself, she knew that if her ex had been there instead, her son would have not benefited in the same way. Her ex was a heavy drinker and spent a lot of time in the pub and would probably not have cared for her son in the same way.

You will know that you are done with this process when you no longer yearn for your situation to be any different.

You will see how the new form serves you and how the old form doesn't.

You will also see how what you perceive to be missing in you may just be 'hiding' somewhere else for the time being, and by doing the little exercise above, you will get to see where it's gone and why.

The grass is NEVER greener; it's just different grass!

The value in seeing the bigger picture

If I had stayed in the relationship with Paul, I would never have known how to embrace my feminine side or take care of myself properly. I would not have been prepared for becoming a mother or healed the wounds I had with my mum. I may not have finally found what I was here to do. I realized that I was here *to support others who were struggling to move on* from their exes, so that *they too could heal and move on.* Why else would I have experienced what I did?

I am not saying that you are destined for the same path. But I have observed with my clients that their exes have pushed them further along their path towards their souls' purpose, leaving them feeling empowered and free.

This is important to remember:

You don't go through what you go through for nothing.

In his book, *The Man's Search for Meaning,* Auschwitz prisoner Victor Frankl shares that what kept him alive was his knowing that he was serving a bigger purpose and that somehow his experience in the concentration camp would someday help others through difficult times.

He surrendered to what was and knew that he had been placed in that unique situation so that he could serve a larger purpose. When the war ended, he wrote his book, which has helped millions around the world to come to terms with what happened, and he ended up helping others to find their own meanings to their lives.

As for my purpose, I know that I went through everything so that I can help you to heal your ex-relationships, so you can fully embrace who you are, in all your glory, by letting go of the anger and resentment. So what bigger purpose are you here to serve? If you are not able to see your purpose right now, that is okay. Just remember that you can always join the dots of your past to make sense of where you are going.

Dissolving regret of the past

"Lay strong foundations for yourself—spiritually, emotionally, physically and mentally and see how the buttons of guilt disappear." ~ **Marina Pearson**

"If only I had done this ... and this ... and this ... then my life would be different and better," I often hear my clients say; but *it is not true!* You don't know anything for sure and it's dangerous to even go there because this sort of thinking just will not serve you.

Regret will eat you up. If you hear yourself saying "if only" then you know that you are still feeling regret about your past and wish that your past had somehow been different. This will drive you mad, have you beating yourself up and will ultimately render you powerless if you continue to entertain the regret. Instead, take the time to challenge your fantasy about how things might have been and ask yourself "What are the good things that have come out of being where I am right now? And what are the factors that would have hindered me if we were still together?"

CASE STUDY: Lauren's story

Lauren came to me as she felt rejected and was very upset that her ex had accused her of being 'too pushy'. She felt that her being too pushy had pushed him away and now felt guilty about having done so, and she wished she hadn't.

Once we went through the process, however, she realized that rather than just being pushy, she was voicing her truth and was pushing for what she wanted. She wanted children and he didn't. She realized that if she hadn't pushed the point, she would have spent many more years in a relationship with a man who didn't want the same things as her and settled for a life she didn't actually want.

If she had not been pushy, she would have found herself not voicing her truth, which would have been a drain on her. She would have wasted her time and wouldn't have gotten clear on what she wanted.

Her being this way now saves her time with any man as she is able to state that she wants a family, and if that person is not similarly minded, she knows she will not wait around. If she had not been pushy in that moment, she would have ended up living her ex's life and not her own.

It served her ex too, as he finally got to express what was going on with him. It gave him the realizations that he needed in order to find happiness in himself. It also helped them both to voice what they wanted. In short, at some unconscious level, they both set this situation up together, to dissolve the denials that were living in both of their hearts. If she hadn't been who she was in that moment, she would have denied herself the life that she truly wanted. Being pushy also helped her not be a doormat. It was an opportunity to set up some boundaries and to say "No—the buck stops here!"

As soon as she got this, the regret about what she had done dissolved and she was able to see the perfection in the moment. Deep gratitude welled up inside of her and her physiology changed.

So, if you feel regret or guilt about what you did or didn't do in the relationship, or that you are not spending enough time with your children ... DON'T! It's all good.

Gratitude to yourself—Be your own best friend

Aside from being able to be grateful for what you have around you, **it's important to be grateful for you.** I cannot reiterate this enough.

Now I know this is something that you may find difficult. You may give your power away to others by giving them the credit, but there is no need. You are the person you have been waiting for. You are amazing just as you are.

If you felt any emotion welling up as you were reading this, then good. It just shows that this magnificent side of you needs attention. A lot of attention!

This quote by Marianne Williamson sums it up for me, which was taken from her book *A Return To Love: Reflections on the Principles of A Course in Miracles:* Thorsons; (Reissue) edition *November 1996*

> "Our deepest fear is not that we are inadequate. Our deepest fear is that we are powerful beyond measure. It is our light, not our darkness that most frightens us. We ask ourselves, Who am I to be brilliant, gorgeous, talented, fabulous? Actually, who are you *not* to be? You are a child of God. You playing small does not serve the world. There is nothing enlightened about shrinking so that other people won't feel insecure around you. We are all meant to shine, as children do. We were born to make manifest the glory of God that is within us. It's not just in some of us; it's in everyone. And as we let our own light shine, we unconsciously give other people permission to do the same. As we are liberated from our own fear, our presence automatically liberates others."
> ~ Marianne Williamson

You are amazing as you are and I know that when you are hurting and angry towards your ex, it is because you have felt rejected in some way. It is difficult to feel this way—it was for me anyway. It took me a long time to understand myself.

After years of being anorexic and not knowing how to look after myself, I finally had to teach myself to start loving myself again.

Looking back now, it seems so amazing and ridiculous that only five years ago I found it so extremely uncomfortable to go to the supermarket to buy myself food on my own, and eating on my own—well, that was even worse! These were harsh reminders that I was single and that I had to look after myself, even though I really didn't want to. I had these ideas in my head that I needed a man to do that for me and that not being in a relationship meant that I had no value.

However, with time, I have grown to understand the following:

People treat me like I treat me.

In other words, if you care for yourself and learn to do lovely things for you, you will treat you better and those around will too.

If you do not acknowledge your wisdom and beauty, others will not acknowledge them. Your internal world is no different from your outer—how you feel on the inside will be reflected in what you attract on the outside.

As you know now—*you don't lack anything. You are wonderful as you are.* Now, if you hear that negative voice in your head going "But, no I am not" then you know that there is still some more work to do! But that's brilliant because this is the biggest gift you could give yourself, the gift of self-love.

A great way to get you into the practice of being grateful is to use a Gratitude Diary or Journal. Here's how...

EXERCISE: Gratitude Journal

1) **Buy a diary**

2) **Write down what you are grateful for that day**—however small—make it at least 10 things.

3) **Do this for 21 days and just observe** what happens—then keep going.

Before your feet touch the ground every morning, say this mantra:

"Life is a gift and I must treasure it, otherwise it won't treasure me."

How are you feeling now? Remember, it's not what happens to you that creates the suffering; it is how you approach your challenges that's important.

As you have learnt, gratitude is so important because it will give you the strength to share and support, as well as, be supported by others.

PART 3: MOVE ON

SUPPORT & SHARE

This last chapter focuses on something that is very dear to my own heart and is the step that makes the most sense to me. This is about ***choosing the right support to share what you are going through.*** You don't have to go through the stress of what you are going through with your ex on your own. I often see women think they can do it on their own and then see them struggle without really needing to. Granted, this comes down to knowing where to go and making sure you are making the right decision.

You don't need to do it on your own

I have often seen women who believe that they will let go of their ex in their own way. Years later they are still angry, resentful and hurt, and although they say they are over it, they are not. I can hear it in their language and in their tone of voice, which is usually cold and antagonistic, and they are still going on about how their ex did this, and how he did that.

Why would you want to do it on your own? It makes no sense to me anymore. I believed I could let go of my baggage on my own, but ten years later nothing had changed, I was still repeating the patterns, and even though I had gone into new relationships and moved on with my life, not having released the hurt from the past did actually take its toll.

Why would you not want to take advantage of experts out there that really know what they are talking about—who have 'been there, done that and got the T-shirt'? You can learn from them and then get to your own destination quicker; but you don't have to be like them. Now you are wise enough to know that there are people like me who can help save you time and money.

I guarantee that you will get your return on your investment and you won't make the same mistake that I did, which was to not address the problem sooner.

Surround yourself with people who will support you

This is so important. I often see women not being able to move on and harbouring the anger as they surround themselves with friends who support their victim story. The only thing this does is to keep them being a victim of their own circumstance and make their 'victim muscle' stronger, disempowering them and making them feel worse. I know people do this, thinking that they are being supportive, and I have been there too. But it makes matters worse not better. It's important to get the right balance here.

There are times for support, but there are also times for a friend to get out the tough love and help her to change how she perceives her situation and how her behaviour may have contributed to it.

Support comes in many shapes and sizes, and although most of these women want it in the way they want it, tough love support can be more helpful. By stepping out from the victim story, they put themselves back into a position of power and are able to change their circumstances.

Women who decide that they are ready to be with other empowered women get through this moment of transition a lot more quickly. It makes sense, right? You become who you surround yourself with. Now, I am not saying that your friends and family won't be a great help when the stress hits; but I do know that they may not be the best people to go to for that help. They will have their own belief systems, with their own opinions, and won't necessarily give you the advice you *need.* And they might instead give you the advice you *want* to hear.

You become who you surround yourself with

It is for that reason that I am setting up *The Divorce Shift Network*, an exclusive community of courageous women who know that they can transform their ex relationships into the catalyst that they need for their own change and growth. The Network runs Meetup groups, online programmes and will have its own Facebook page.

When I was going through my own divorce, the one thing that saved me was the Meetup group that I discovered in New York City. They seemed to understand what I was going through, and being around people who could empathise with my situation definitely stopped me feeling isolated. I am, in fact, in deep gratitude for this group of souls who really looked after me. I was finding it very difficult to sleep and was terrified of sleeping alone because I felt so depressed and lonely. One of the group members came to my rescue and would sit with me at night, just to make sure that I fell asleep. I honestly don't know what I would have done without them.

Although this time was a time of deep pain and anguish, I also experienced a profound generosity and a side to humankind that was unbeknown to me. It was amazing to experience this coming together of strangers, who were in such deep pain, to help one another get through. I am indebted to them as they kept me safe and made sure that I was okay.

Now I am part of different communities that keep me accountable, but who also have supported me in becoming more of who I am, as well as fulfilling my potential as a woman. Most of my friends now are entrepreneurs and I have shaken loose from many friends of the past who were not necessarily a part of my picture anymore. I felt like I had outgrown them, or at least that we had grown in different directions. Has that ever happened to you?

I see this with my clients too. In just five short sessions I can see their transformation as they let go of past baggage and unpack it. I came to realize that I wanted to create a one-stop shop where you could come and share and feel supported by others, while learning, healing and awakening to a new perspective.

CASE STUDY: A story about Alicia

Alicia came to me as she was obsessing about her ex, who she still had to see. She had been struggling for almost a year to get over him and had had to leave her community to remove herself from him. Once she thought she was over him, she went back and realized that she was still having her buttons pushed by him.

We decided to do a short stint together to see how it would go and after just five sessions her obsessing stopped. She felt free and started dating again because she wanted to, not because she felt she had to.

It turned out that six weeks later she was dating other men, feeling extremely loved and fulfilled, and she was friends with her ex. Now, of course hers is one of the special cases. I am not saying that in five or ten weeks you will be over it and free. It all depends on who you are and how much work you put into it; but it does not have to take a lifetime for you to heal from your break-up.

Time to empower YOU

In the previous chapter we shared about how important it is to take care of yourself. This final chapter now is about empowering yourself and doing so from the place of your *feminine power*. The major transitions that you have had to experience since your divorce or break-up may have uprooted your sense of who you are and will probably have knocked all your confidence out of you. The good news is that *you can now use this time to take charge of your life in all of its areas!*

Empowering yourself in all the areas of your life is a fundamental key to reclaiming your inner mojo, feeling your confidence return and knowing who you are.

The women I meet who went through their divorce or break-up and had to deal with their exes, just like you, and are now celebrating life, are the ones who did the work and decided that it was time to empower their life.

What is empowerment and why is it so important?

The dictionary defines empowerment as 't*he giving or delegation of power or authority; authorization*'.

When you are looking at it from the perspective of empowering yourself, it means *to give yourself the power or authority*. The way I see it, you give yourself the authority in all the seven areas of your life. I learnt this from one of my fabulous teachers, Dr John Demartini, who explained that there are seven areas of your life that you need to master to be truly empowed.

The seven areas of your life are:

Financial: How you manage your money, what you invest it in, how you save it.

Social: The sorts of people you hang out with, the opportunities you get to surround yourself with, the sorts of people you want to hang out with.

Vocational: Whether you are the expert in your field and whether you are successful at what you do.

Familial: This refers to the area of family and/or people you regard as family.

Mental: This refers to solving problems, learning, thinking, creativity.

Physical: This refers to your physical well-being, your energy force, your vitality.

Spiritual: This can refer to your connection with yourself, or whatever you deem as spiritual.

The key here is to be your very own 'hostess with the mostess' in every area of your life, so ***you can be the authority in it.***

Chances are that what you do not control will control you. So think about where you feel somebody else is controlling the strings—is it financially, for instance?

Where do you feel you could have more control?

The areas that are of most value to you tend to be the ones where you are already empowered—they are your 'home turf'. Being a hard-working professional, for example, immediately gives you empowered authority in the work area of your life. If you have kids then maybe it's in your family. Either way, the goal is to empower *every* area. As a woman of the 21st Century, your own sense of confidence and authority is the key to you not being so caught up with your ex and what he is, or is not, up to as he will have less power over you.

Let me give you an example: I often see women who have separated and are still fully dependent on their ex for money in one way or another. Money is the main reason why disagreements take place and why conflict arises. Does this sound familiar? So whether you have children to fend for, or are running a business together with your ex, taking responsibility for knowing what to do and how to manage things will be the key to empowering yourself in this area.

I wasn't self-empowered either. In fact, let's just say that I was disempowered in the majority of my seven areas. I felt I was being pushed and pulled without knowing which way to turn, like a leaf in the wind. I had decisions made for me and I felt lost. I really didn't know who I was, nor did I understand the power I had within me.

By doing a lot of work on myself, I was able to get myself up to a level where I now look after my finances by working with a mentor. I look after my health by taking the necessary action to ensure it. I develop my mental capacity by learning and going to workshops and working with experts in their field. I was broken spiritually and was not able to connect with myself nor with the environment around me, which left me with a constant feeling of distrust and loss. However, now I connect with myself often and am more in touch with my abilities to connect and tune in.

I would never have imagined that as a result of the hard work and tenacity to create the life I want for myself *that I actually would!* My circle of friends has changed and the kind of people I now relate to are all running successful businesses and are extremely well-connected, very wealthy and making a difference in the world.

I now run my own business and never in a month of Sundays would I have imagined that I would be speaking, writing a number of books, or even being interviewed by newspapers and national magazines! I am also in a loving relationship with a man who is everything I could desire and more. He is a proper gentleman who I can feel settled with and loved by. We are planning now for a family in the not too distant future.

I don't say this to brag. I just want to illustrate that you too can also have whatever you want, in whatever shape or form you want it. I am not saying that I have arrived — far from it! I still know that I am capable of so much more and everyday there is something new to learn and grow from.

So, how do you even start to empower these areas of your life?

Well, for me it was a gradual thing. I went to seminars like *Millionaire Mind Intensive* with T Harv Eker, to learn about how to manage my money and grow my wealth, and the *Keeping the Love You Find* workshop, to learn about conscious relationships. I went to *The Breakthrough* with Dr John Demartini to learn about how to embrace both my shadow and my light and also went to *The Breakthrough to Success* with Christopher Howard, to discover how to manage my mind. I have learned many lessons in business, speaking and personal life through attending other seminars, like with Clinton Swaine and many more.

Did I spend a lot of money? Yes; however, I knew that I needed things to change.

It all started with my exes and that is why I am so grateful to each of them, as they really were the catalysts towards my changes and my on-going healing journey.

If you look at the most successful people out there, they have worked for what they've got and have taken the time to commit to the needed processes to get there.

As you will agree, there is life beyond your ex and divorce. It really is *a new chapter of your life!* Yes, things may well not be as you want them to be and you may be struggling with moving on; but the more you surround yourself with like-minded others who can support you on your journey, the easier it will be.

I would say "Dare to dream and go for it."

As Stephen Covey once said, "Live out of your imagination, not your history."

Now you may be thinking *Can I truly create from my imagination?*

And the answer is 'yes'. If you can think it, it is possible. As Walt Disney said, "If you can dream it, you can do it."

So how do you even start to get your creative juice flowing when you may not even know what you want? Here is a guide.

EXERCISE:

Step 1: Find out what you want to create

Ask yourself "If money was not an option and I was to have the perfect day, how would I live it?"

(This will get your imagination going and give you huge insights into what you value and what you find important. Keep writing all the ideas that come to you.)

Step 2: Create a vision board

Buy some magazines and cut out the images that represent what you want to create and what you wish to include in your life. Now stick them on a piece of cardboard.

Keep the vision board in sight so that you see it every day.

(Why do this at all? Because your unconscious part of your brain runs 95 per cent of your results and it only understands pictures—you are training it to see what it wants.)

Be sure to have fun while doing it and get your kids involved to help you so that it now becomes a fun family project. By living in the land of possibility and asking yourself "What are the steps I need to take to get there?" you will stop focusing on what was and will not get so dragged down by your ex, so you can focus on *what can be*.

So where would you rather be living? In the land of possibility and plenty?

Part of moving on is being able to truly acknowledge who you are and what you want – so make it your sole purpose over the next coming months to do just that.

Embrace your feminine

I have spoken about empowering the seven areas of your life and how you can do this. The next step is about being able to embrace your feminine side—who you are as a woman.

Now, you may be thinking, *Hey, but I do embrace it*

If so, that's great!

In any event, it would still be useful for you to gauge how much time *you live in it,* as when we women are dealing with stress, we tend to live more and more in our masculine aspect and neglect or ignore our feminine side.

Embracing your feminine energy can really help you let go of the sore points between you and your ex. It can help you surrender more to how things are, and to just relax and have fun in the mystical space of the unknown.

You do need both polarities — masculine and feminine — and what I found is that the more you live in your masculine, the more you will want to control and know what the outcome will be. This can make the 'moving on' part very difficult, which is why it is important that you learn to bring in more balance.

The differences between your masculine and feminine

Masculine Energy	Feminine Energy
Masculine energy is outward-thrusting, directed, focused, goal-oriented and productive.	Feminine energy is inward-drawing, creative, process-oriented, unstructured, and procreative.
Corresponds with linear, left-brained thinking and with doing.	Corresponds with big picture, right-brained thinking, and with being.
Characterized by exertion and forced penetration.	Characterized by repose and willing absorption.
Structures and organizes the environment.	Conditions and nurtures the environment.

Focusses on a single project at a time with the objective of outer world productivity. Laser beam-like, completely focused.	More concerned with generating inner world atmosphere and possibility, with focus in many different directions. Radiant in all directions at once.
Intent on competition, erection and conquest: Skyscrapers, bridges, super-tankers, space shuttles, drilling for oil, mining for precious metals.	Intent on cooperation, nurturing and improvement, deconstruction and yielding: Nursing, education, support services.
Characterized by logic, reason, sensibility and cause & effect thinking (if this, then that).	Characterized by the illogical, the unreasonable and the nonsense. No specific linear cause & effect thinking.
Limited by the known world.	Inspired by the unknown world.
Relies on measurement, proof, engineering, architecture and science.	Relies on intuition, instinct, emotion and feelings, metaphysics, noetic science and spirituality.

So why is it so important to embrace your feminine self and live there more often than staying in your masculine? Because you will find that you will feel less stressed, and will not end up burnt out. Spending more time in an energy that is not your natural aspect will put unnecessary strain on you.

By consciously staying in your feminine, you allow him to step up as a man. In addition, it will give you all the essentials to work through this tricky time. Being able to go into a place of trust, surrender and willingness to let go of the control will repay itself time and time again. It will also give you the opportunity to get excited about the unknown.

Maybe by now you are thinking *Well, how is it possible for me to live in my feminine energy, to just let go and trust that everything will turn out fine? ... And how is it possible for me to appreciate him and surrender when I cannot even trust him?* To do that will take practise and the first step is to connect with yourself.

Go quietly within

Go quietly within. Connect with yourself on a daily basis through **meditation**. By connecting with yourself regularly, you will be practising to create more of an inner world and will feel calmer as a result. I have found this to be the key to maintaining an inner calm.

Meditation has a lot of benefits. Not only will it calm the mind, but it will also reduce the stress you feel and will give you the opportunity to lower anxieties if you are having them.

Use **breathing techniques** to slow down and soften your experience of life, which can lead to increasing your trust levels of yourself and those around you. It will also help you with the stress and your sleep.

"***Breath is the bridge which connects life to consciousness, which unites your body to your thoughts. Whenever your mind becomes scattered, use your breath as the means to take hold of your mind again."*** **~ Thich Nhat Hanh, *The Miracle of Mindfulness***

I have practised yoga for over twelve years now, and I have come to realize how important the breath is to our well-being. Shallow breathing is usually associated with depression while deep breaths will get the right amount of oxygen to each part and organ in the body, giving you energy and vitality in an instant and quietening your mind.

A great breathing technique that you can use is one that I show you on the video at <www.GoodByeMrEx.com/BreathingTechnique>. This technique of breathing from the diaphragm is really important to let go of the tension, but will also help you to connect with yourself.

Choosing when you go into your feminine and surrendering to what is, while dancing into the unknown, is very powerful and incredibly empowering. It will give you a sense of freedom, as you will no longer need or want to control your surroundings.

A final note to say thank you and well done!

Well, it looks like you have finally reached your destination! Like a traveller, you have kept yourself open and inquisitive in your journey through this process and now it has come time to say goodbye, for now.

All I wish to say is "Thank you". Thank you for taking the time out to care enough about you and your growth, and for letting me be here with you to help lead you through it. Well done for taking the Seven Steps that will finally have you expressing yourself, releasing and moving on.

When you commit to the process of moving on and discover your 'whys', getting over your fears will be much easier and you will, in fact, be more than halfway there. Expressing your emotions fully as part of this commitment is key to letting go of them and giving you your vital energy back. By embracing your ex as part of you, the judgments and resentments will dissolve, liberating you of any heavy feelings you are currently experiencing. Finding the good in your negative story will help you see the gifts that you may have not been aware of, giving you back your power. As you now know, you will also need to unravel your unconscious story if you want to stop your ex from pushing your buttons.

Do remember that rejection is never personal and that your ex is his own person, with his own triggers and ways of doing things. Interpreting why he has done what he has done without the inquiring will keep you frustrated; so inquiry is the best remedy for this.

Make sure you focus on your internal world, your language and how you communicate, so that you decrease the inner and outer conflict you may feel. But the most powerful and simple aspect of the steps is your commitment to your daily practice of gratitude. Writing in your gratitude journal will take you into your sacred sanctuary of gifts and peace—where time stops and you are present with the here and now.

Don't forget that, yes, you can do all of this on your own. But you can also seek to be supported by a group of women and someone qualified who can teach you the proactive approach to leave your past behind you, dance into the future and create a new life full of possibilities.

The biggest gift you can give yourself and others is that of empowering yourself—and then you can do the same for those around you. It takes a certain special type of woman to embrace the seven S.H.I.F.T. steps that I have placed before you, and you are obviously that sort of woman; otherwise, you would not have read this book.

I believe that you can transform anything if you choose to. It still may not seem that way right now, but, really, you can! Every negative moment in your life can become the moment to transform your life. Each of these moments are blessings—stepping stones bringing you closer to your path of purpose and passion. The trick is to just stay calm, be present and connect with your true power.

The one thing I do know is that you have a choice. You always have a choice to either stay stuck, or move forward. Give yourself the gift today of choosing to truly embrace your power—so you can then gift that power to others. There is nothing more inspiring than seeing other women turn their lives around, and, in turn, help others do the same. You can turn something that was *in* your way to something that helps you move *along* your way!

See this as a new chapter of your life—a new opportunity to embrace *all of who you are*, so that you can live the life you want for yourself! You deserve that, don't you? Do you not deserve to close your eyes and just say "Thank you" to each of your exes for having been in your life, so that you can free yourself of the pain of the past? So that you can build the foundations now for your future?

Gratitude is a wonderful thing and will nurture you and empower you along your journey of life. I wish you the very best along yours as you move on. May you be empowered and live in happy appreciation of the wonderful life you are already living and the life of your dreams you aspire to!

Marina Pearson

Bibliography

Braden, Gregg. The Divine Matrix: Bridging Time, Space, Miracles, and Belief: USA: Hay House; First Edition first Printing edition (January 2, 2008)

Chopra, Deepak. Debbie Ford, Marianne Williamson The Shadow Effect: Illuminating the Hidden Power of Your True Self: USA: HarperOne; Reprint edition (May 3, 2011)

Ford, Debbie. The Dark Side of The Light Chasers: USA: Penguin, 2010.

Frankl, E Victor. Man's Search For Meaning: The classic tribute to hope from the Holocaust: Rider; New edition (6 May 2004)

Katie, Byron. Loving What Is: Four Questions That Can Change Your Life: USA: Three Rivers Press (December 23, 2003)

Lipton, Bruce. The Biology of Belief: Unleashing the Power of Consciousness, Matter, & Miracles: USA: Hay House; Revised edition (2008)

Williamson, Marianne. A Return to Love: Reflections on the Principles of "A Course in Miracles": USA: Harper Paperbacks; Reissue edition (March 15, 1996)

About the Author

Marina is an inspirational speaker, author and the founder of Divorce Shift, an organization that supports women who are struggling to get over their ex relationships with highly interactive online workshops, creating a powerful community of women so that they can express release and move on in the comfort of their own homes.

She has been featured in the UK tabloids such as **The Guardian** and **The Daily Mail**, while being featured in women's magazines discussing matters of divorce and her own journey.

Marina has been there, done that, got the T-Shirt and written the book. She went through her own divorce, is the daughter of a divorcee and has been through a countless number of breakups.

Because of these unique experiences and having worked with a growing number of clients, she has experienced the detrimental effects that hanging onto ex relationships can have on the individual as well as on their family and children.

Marina is also the author of ***It's Your Right to Be Wrong In Relationships*** and a number of e-books.

www.DivorceShift.com

Lightning Source UK Ltd.
Milton Keynes UK
UKOW050833291112

202914UK00004B/8/P